Emma Bo

1,106 Fascinating Fa(

© 2014, Emma Boyes
emmaboyes@gmail.com

ALL RIGHTS RESERVED. This book contains material protected under International and Federal Copyright Laws and Treaties. Any unauthorized reprint or use of this material is prohibited. No part of this book may be reproduced or transmitted in any form or by any means, electronic or mechanical, including photocopying, recording, or by any information storage and retrieval system without express written permission from the author.

With thanks to:

Damon Torsten Nash, Lauren Pears and all at Lady Dinah's Cat Emporium, Rebecca Hall at Nine Lives Greece, Christina and Joan at Santorini Animal Welfare Association

Cats not only have whiskers on their feet,
but also behind their front paws.
These help her walk on uneven ground
and feel the size of her prey.

Cat have blood types like people do – they
can be A, B or AB. Most cats are blood type A.

An adult cat has
230 bones in her body.
Humans have 206.

Ten per cent of a cat's bones are in her tail.

Cats have five toes on their front paws
but only four on their back.

The domestic cat can
run at a speed of 31mph.
The world record holder for the fastest
100 metre sprint in our world,
Usain Bolt, can only reach 27mph.

Usain's record is 9.58 seconds
for a hundred metre run.
In August 2012, a cheetah
made it in 5.95 seconds.

Cats' normal body temperature
is 100-102.5 F.
A human's is 98.6 F.

500,000 cats were enlisted in the war effort
by the British in World War One.
Their mission?
To act as mousers in the trenches.

A group of cats is called a clowder.
A group of kittens is a kindle.

Cats can most easily recognise a name
that ends in an 'e' sound,
for example Blackie or Fluffy.

Tortoiseshell cats are almost always female.

In the rare case that a male tortoiseshell
cat is born, he will be sterile.

Ginger cats are almost always male.

It's estimated that less than one in fifty
ginger kitties is female.

Only between 50 and 75 per cent of cats
actually react to catnip.
It's believed to be an inherited trait.

The first cat show was held at
Crystal Palace in England in 1871.

Contrary to popular belief,
you shouldn't actually give
cats cows' milk to drink.
Most cats are lactose intolerant.

Unlike humans, cats cannot
survive on a vegan or vegetarian diet.

Cats are 'true' or 'obligate' carnivores'.
Humans, in comparison, are omnivores.

Around 10 percent of the
population are allergic to cats.

A third of the people
who are allergic to cats
still own at least one cat.

Almost all white cats with
blue eyes are completely deaf.

If a cat has one blue eye,
he is usually deaf on that side of his head, too.

Domestic cats in Australia have not been
free to roam since the mid
1990s, when various
laws were passed in various states
restricting their movements.
This is to protect Australian wildlife.

Cats can move each ear independently,
which allows them to hear sounds
coming from two different directions at once.

Australia and Antarctica are
the only two places in the world
without any kind of native cat population.

It is believed cats came to Australia
from ships where they acted as mousers.

A cat's night vision
is six times better than our own.

Cats were highly regarded
by the Ancient Egyptians.
So much so, that killing a cat was
a crime punishable by death.

Neutered cats live two to three years longer
than unneutered ones.

The average lifespan for a
feral cat is 3 – 5 years,
whereas a domestic cat can
live to age 16 or even older.

Cats have a keen sense of smell,
heightened by the Jacobson's Organ,
which allows them to 'taste' smells.

Most cats don't have eyelashes.

Cats don't have a collarbone,
and this allows them to squeeze into
numerous tight spots. As long as they can
fit their heads through the opening,
they can get their whole
body through, too.

Cats can get sunburn.

A feline pregnancy lasts about two months.

A litter will generally be made up
of between one to nine kittens.

Cats can't see things that are
directly under their nose – literally.

Adult cats have 30 teeth. Kittens have 26.

Just like humans, kittens have baby teeth
which are replaced with
their permanent gnashers
at around three months.

Kittens don't have molars.

Kittens' milk teeth are brittle and
break easily.

Kitten's teeth are also
tiny – the smallest
measuring about half
a centimetre in length,
including the root.

EVERYTHING YOU'VE EVER WANTED TO KNOW ABOUT CAT CAFES

A cat café is simply somewhere people can go and drink coffee which has resident cats.

Although cat cafes are often associated with Japan, the first cat café in the world was actually opened in Taipei in Taiwan in 1998.

This café became very popular with Japanese tourists, and it was no surprise when, in 2004, the first cat café was opened in Japan in Osaka.

There are now at least 39 cat cafes in Tokyo. The first to open was Cat's Store in 2005.

There are now cat cafes in
Korea, Malaysia, Bangkok,
Singapore, Dubai, Austria,
Hungary, Germany,
Spain, France, Lithuania, Italy,
the US and Canada.

Australia's first cat café – Cat
Café Melbourne – is
due to open in July 2014.

The first cat café in the UK was
the Totnes Cat Café,
which opened in South
Devon in May 2013.
Sadly, in early 2014, it had to close due
to the owner's ill health.

Lady Dinah's Cat Emporium opened
in Shoreditch, London in March 2014,
after a successful
crowdfunding campaign on Indiegogo.

After seeing this become a huge success,
many other
cat cafes are now being planned
in other areas of the UK.

A male cat is called a Tom and
a female is known as a Queen or a Molly.

The official name for a cat lover is an ailurophile.

Likewise, a cat hater is called an ailurophobe.

The technical word for a hairball is a bezoar.

Cats can be 'left pawed' or 'right pawed',
just like humans are left or right handed.

Most female cats are right pawed,
while males tend to favour their left.

The first cat in space was called Felicette.
The French sent the intrepid feline into space in 1963.

A cat can jump up to five times its own height.

To this day, no one is really sure how a cat purrs.

Isaac Newton, along with the law of relativity,
also invented the cat flap.

Cats' jaws cannot move sideways.

The majority of cats were of the
short haired varieties until about 100 years ago.

Every cat has a unique 'nose print'
just like humans have unique finger prints.

A cat's heart beats almost twice as fast as ours,
at a speed of between 110 to 140 beats per minute.

Cats can only sweat through their paw pads.

A cats' back paws aren't as long or as sharp
as her front claws as they don't retract.

Cats can hear ultrasonic sounds.
So can rodents, but dogs and humans lack this ability.

A cat purrs at the same frequency as
an idling diesel engine – about 26 purrs a second.

A cat called Smokey, who lives in Pitsford,
can purr as loud as a lawnmower and
louder than a vacuum cleaner.

Other animals that purr are guinea pigs,
rabbits, lemurs, squirrels, elephants and
gorillas, although the sounds they all produce
are very different.

There are some 500 million domestic cats worldwide.

The word **CAT** in various languages…

Armenian: Gatz
Arabic: biss
Basque: catua
Bulgarian: kotka
Chinese: mio
Czech: kocka
Dutch: kat
Egyptian: mau
Estonian: kass
Finnish: kissa
French: chat
German: katze
Greek: catta
Hawiian: popoki
Hindu: katas
Icelandic: kottur
Indonesian: qitta
Italian: gatto
Japanese: neko
Latin: cattus
Lithuanian: katinas
Malay: kucing
Maltese: qattus
Slovak: macka

Spanish/Portugese: gato
Swahili: paka
Swedish/Norwegian: katt
Polish: kot
Romanian: pisica
Russian: koshka
Ukranian: kotuk
Thai/Vietnamese: meo
Turkish: kedi
Yiddish: kats

Stroking a cat lowers your blood pressure.

Around 50 percent of cat owners
have never taken their cat to a vet.

It may be difficult to tell the difference between
dog and cat food, but a cat that eats only dog food
may eventually go blind. This is because dog food
does not contain the substance Taurine,
which cats need.

Taurine is also found in energy drinks like Red Bull.

Almost all cats adore eating tuna,
despite the fact that these massive fish
are in no way part of their natural diet.

Cats can reliably predict earthquakes.

Cats are naturally nocturnal animals.

Cats are currently the most popular house pet
in both the US and UK.

Most cut flowers are extremely poisonous to cats.

A full list of poisonous plants is at the end of this book, but some common ones to watch out for are lilies, daffodils, tulips, snowdrops and lily of the valley.

There are about 60,000 hairs on per square inch on the back of a cat and 120,000 on his fluffy belly.

The band Procol Harum (famous for the hit Nights In White Satin) was named by manager Guy Stevens after a friend's pedigree Burmese cat.

After many journalists tried to track down the kitty in question unsuccessfully, it became one of the most bizarre rock and roll mysteries ever.

In 2006, writer Ian Marchant released a book called The Longest Crawl, and claimed on his travels around Wales, he met with a man called Ash, who claimed to have dealt acid to the band and to have owned the Burmese in question.

Betty Boo's 1990 hit Where Are You Baby? was actually written about her lost cat.

Buzzfeed has a weekly newsletter that you can sign up for dedicated just to cats.

Cats do not only purr when they are happy, but also when they are in great pain, giving birth or nursing.

Purring seems to be similar
to a kind of meditation for felines.

Purring may aid in healing bones,
tendons, ligaments and muscles and provide
cats with pain relief.
We simply don't know enough
about it to determine for sure.

Cats can be trained just like dogs.
They can be taught to,
for example, come, fetch, sit,
beg and jump through hoops.
It just requires different tactics.

The more you chat to your cat,
the more she will 'talk' back to you.
Likewise, cats soon lose interest in communicating
with unresponsive owners.

95 per cent of cat owners admit to talking
to their cat. Personally,
I think the other 5 per cent
are just too embarrassed to admit to it.

Around 21 per cent of dogs
and 7 per cent of cats snore.

Cats also suffer from many 'human' diseases
like feline versions of AIDS, cancer and diabetes.

Female cats can be sexually mature
by five months,
whereas males won't be for at least
nine months to a year.

There have been found to be no disadvantages
to neutering a cat at any

age from three months old,
as long as they are strong
enough for the surgery.

Cats sleep a lot of the time.
Males tend to sleep more than females,
and can clock up 20 hours sleep in a day.
The average
for a domesticated cat
is about 16 hours a day.

No one really understands
why cats need to sleep so
much. Even house cats,
who hardly lead stressful
or exhaustingly active lives,
sleep most of the time.

Cats are incredibly good at killing snakes.

Lots of cats are partial to parsley.

92 per cent of cats are moggies.

In the US, there is no real word for 'moggy'.

According to a 2000 survey,
only 36 per cent of cats
sleep with their owners on their beds.
It wasn't reported whether this was the human's
choice or the cat's.

TAMA, STATION MASTER CAT

If you look closely at this train station in
Kinokawa, south eastern Japan, you'll notice that
it's shaped like a cat's face.

Kishi station was not a well used one as it is
in a quiet rural village, and in 2004
it was facing closure.

Tama was a calico stray cat that lived with some other strays near Kishi station.

In 2007, the station was still not doing well, and with most trains running empty, the decision was made to make all the station staff redundant to cut costs.

In 2007, railway line officials made Tama station master and even provided her with a uniform as an idea to try to attract visitors.

Tama is paid in cat food and now has a home to call her own.

Two of Tama's fellow strays, a ginger cat called Miiko and a ginger and white called Chibi, were also employed as her assistants. Since then, Miiko has gone to kitty heaven.

Tama has her own official office, which is a converted ticket booth where she can take a nap.

In 2010, the boring old train station building was demolished and the new, kitty shaped one built in its place.

Inside the new station building is a cat-themed café and a souvenir shop which sells things like Tama t-shirts, mugs, fans, books, pens and much more.

The Wakayama Electric Railway, which currently runs the line, now operates three themed trains – there's a Strawberry Train, a Toy Train, and of course, a cat-themed Tama Train.

Tama now has an apprentice called Nitama (Tama Two or Tama The Second) to share her hefty responsibilities and take over the job when she's ready to retire.

Since Tama's appointment as Station Master, Kishi station has become extremely popular, with most of its visitors under the age of 12.

Most vets in the UK will neuter a kitten from five
or six months old.

Cats move so gracefully because
they first move their two left feet,
then their two right.
The only other animals that do
this are giraffes and camels.

Cats have backward pointing spikes
on their tongues to help them groom themselves.

When they're born, kittens are absolutely
helpless and cannot even see or hear.

Kittens open their eyes at around five days
and start walking at around two weeks old.

All kittens, like human babies,
are born with blue eyes.
But as they grow up, their eye colour,
also like human children,
almost always changes.

Even many solid coloured
cats have tabby markings,

which you can see if
you look hard enough.

Cats are Britain's most popular pet.
There are 7.7 million pet cats compared
to 6.6 million pet dogs.

A cat has 24 whiskers on her face,
12 on either side of her nose.

In 2005, 13 million calendars featuring cats were sold.

There are numerous dogs depicted in cave
paintings, but not a single feline.

In case you were wondering, the
reason there are no cave paintings of cats
is that they became domesticated much later on
than other animals like goats, cows and dogs.

If there was a house fire in Ancient Egypt,
residents would be sure to save the cat
before anyone or anything else.

Before domesticating cats, the Egyptians first
tried taming hyenas
to deal with their rodent
problem. That didn't really work out,
so they moved
on to cats, who seemed to be more
amenable to the idea.

Ancient Egyptians also used cats as 'hunting dogs'.

In 1888, some 800,000 mummified cat bodies
were found, and sold to a fertilizer company for $18.43 a ton.

The Japanese once believed that
owning a cat was inhumane.

In 1602, a Japanese law stated that all house cats
were free spirits and should be released.

The Ancient Incas also worshipped cats.

During the Middle Ages in Western Europe,
doctors would prescribe cats to the insane in
the belief that having a mog would cure them
of their ills.

During the Renaissance, practically
every home in England had at least one cat in it.

The first American to own a cat was Lucy Hayes,
the wife of President Rutherford B. Hayes.

The first domestic cat in America was a present
from the Ambassador of Siam,
and was called (rather unimaginatively) Siam.

Cats and the Royal Navy have a long history
together, but in 1974 they were banned
from Navy ships.

The PDSA Dickin Medal for valour
shown by animals
has only been awarded to one cat.

That puss was called Simon, and he was given
the award posthumously in 1949 for his time
serving on board the HMS Amethyst. Although
wounded by a shell blast, he continued his
rat-catching duties with due diligence.

Old female cats are called Grimalkins.

Like humans, there are slightly more female cats
than male. Around 51 per cent of felines are lady cats.

About forty per cent of people who own dogs
also own at least one cat as well.

The average number of cats that cat owners have is 2.1.

According to figures, it's estimated that only
around 21 per cent of cats are adopted from rescue centres.

The first cloned kitten
was born on December 22, 2001.

When a cat rubs her head against you
or the furniture to mark it with her scent,
it's called 'bunting'.

Cats spend about one third of their
waking lives grooming themselves.
No one can accuse them of
not keeping up appearances.

A good mouser can easily kill
over a thousand mice in a year.

Feral cats have two different coats – a
thick, plush one for the Winter months,
and a lighter one for the Summer.

They typically shed their Winter coat in Spring
and their Summer coats in the Autumn.

However, since domesticated cats have a
warm environment all year round,
pet cats shed some fur all year round, too. Yay!

Pedigree cats, particularly Siamese and Burmese,
enjoy sucking and chewing wool.
No one knows why these specific breeds
are partial to the taste.

Cats don't like the sensation of
blowing air as it reminds them of hissing.

Cats are adept at climbing - up, at least.
They use their back paws to grip.
They get stuck because they can't figure out that
they need to go down backwards
rather than face first.

Despite the popular myth,
the fire brigade (in the UK, at least)
will generally NOT
rush to the aid of a hapless feline
stranded up a tree.
I know because I've called and asked.

Wild cats won't always sleep in the same
place and don't have a 'den' as such,
which is probably
why pet cats like to mix up
their sleeping spots.

If you want a cat to stop purring, turn on a tap.

During the Blitz, many cat owners
noticed that their cats would run away and hide
when an air raid was about to happen – even
before the warning sirens sounded.

Cats are crepuscular – meaning that they
are at their most active at twilight.

CAT PEOPLE VS DOG PEOPLE

The University of Texas undertook a study in 2010 into the personality differences between cat and dog people. They quizzed 4,565 people for the survey.

Despite their increasing popularity as pets, only 12 per cent of people identified themselves as a 'cat person' compared to 46 per cent who identified as a 'dog person'.

Almost 28 per cent said they were both and 15 percent didn't think of themselves as either.

People who prefer dogs to cats tend to be more sociable, extroverted and outgoing, whereas as cat people are more creative, open and neurotic.

Dog people were also 13 per cent more agreeable and 11 per cent more conscientious.

Although both cat and dog people were more likely to hold a degree, cat people are 17 per cent more likely to have a post-graduate degree. That makes us smarter, right?

A 2008 Gallup survey of 2,000 Americans found that 33 per cent of dog owners identified as Republican compared to only 28 per cent of cat owners.

Dog people were 30 per cent more likely to live in the country and 24 per cent more likely to have children.

A psychological study by Gosling, Sandy and Potter in 2010 found that people believed very different things about cat and dog people.

A typical dog person was said to be "loyal, direct, kind, faithful, utilitarian, helpful and a team player".

Cat people, however, were "graceful, subtle, independent, intelligent, thoughtful and mysterious".

If you're a cat man, you're more likely to be lucky in love, especially with women. Ninety per cent of women said they thought men who owned cats were nicer and more sensitive than those without.

According to VW, cat owners are more environmentally friendly than dog owners, as a cat's carbon footprint is more like a VW Golf, whereas a dog's is more like a Hummer.

A Hunch.com survey dug even deeper when they quizzed some 700,000 people about their pets and themselves.

It found that cat people were more common in Europe and Oceania, whereas dog people were more likely to be based in North or South America.

In a perhaps less surprising fact given the nature of dog ownership, dog people were 36 per cent more likely to be active outdoors.

Cat people were 21 per cent more likely to try and rescue a stray kitten themselves, whereas dog people were 67 per cent more likely to call animal control, the RSPCA or equivalent.

The survey even quizzed them about their favourite Beatle. Dog owners were 18 per cent more likely to prefer Paul, and cat owners were 25 per cent more likely to prefer George.

Cat people are 21 per cent more likely to enjoy ironic humour and puns, whereas dog people are 30 per cent more likely to find slapstick humour and impressions tickle their funnybone.

Dog people are 33 per cent more likely to use a picture of their pet or child as a picture on Facebook rather than one of themselves.

Both cat and dog people tend to be optimists.

Despite the stereotypical image of the crazy cat lady, the good news is that cat and dog people are both just as likely to be married or in a long term relationship.

Cat people are less likely to like children than dog owners. Only 30 per cent of cat owners say they like them, as opposed to 48 percent of dog owners.

About 70 per cent of the time,
cats are sleeping lightly. They are only very rarely
experiencing REM sleep.

A cat will stretch out to sleep when it is hot
and curl up to sleep when it is cooler.

Not all cats hate the water - Turkish Vans
for instance, are quite famous
for being able swimmers.

Some dogs, like humans, are
prone to motion sickness.
However, cats are never afflicted.

Most cats run at the first sign of the
vacuum cleaner, but some strange felines
seem to enjoy being vacuumed!

Every cat's purr is unique.

Cats' eyes have a reflective layer
called the tapetum.

Cats have an extra eyelid
called the nictitating membrane.
It shuts horizontally.

However, if you can see the
nictitating membrane,
it generally means the cat in
question is unwell.

Cats can hear a wider range of
sounds than humans.
They can hear in the range of around
10 octaves, whereas we only have
8.5 octaves range.

Under a microscope, you can see that
a cat's tongue is covered in mini barbs.

Cats cannot taste sweet things.

A cat who is hungry won't hunt as well as
one who is well fed.

A cat can eat up to 20 mice a day.

When cats wash their bodies straight after
you have touched them, it's believed that they
are doing it to 'process' your scent, not to
remove your smell from them, as some people think.

Kittens in the womb
grow their whiskers before their fur.

Lower upper lip whiskers (the longer ones)
are called mystacials,
and the shorter whiskers on the chin
are called mandibulars.

Male cats also have teats.

Although cats can sprint very fast,
they can only do this in short bursts.

A cat can jump six times her own length.

The latin name for the
domestic cat is Felis catus.

The tabby is the 'natural' colouring
of the domestic cat. If people
were to stop breeding specific types of cats
the majority of felines would eventually become
short haired black and ginger tabbies.

Siamese cats are likely to have really come
from Siam (Thailand) and the Burmese
from Burma, but some other breed names,
confusingly, seem to have nothing to do
with their country of origin.

In Thailand
(the country formerly known as Siam),
Siamese cats are called Chinese cats.

Russian Blue cats were once called Archangel cats.

Sphynx cats are not actually completely hairless.
They have a soft coat of 'vellus' fur.

Sphynx cats need to be bathed
once a week, much to their chagrin.

The Rex breeds of cats have a curly coat.

Ragdoll cats are so called because they
go limp like a rag doll when they are held.

Munchkin cats have short legs
and are the feline version of the dachshund.

Cats' coats can go grey with age
just as human hair can.

Black cats can also 'rust'
and their fur turn a reddish brown
if they spend a lot of time out in the sun.

Cats can have food allergies, just like people.

It's also believed that mogs can suffer
from IBS (irritable bowel syndrome).

Some people believe that you can 'paw read'
cats in the same way that you can
palm read people.

Apparently, the dewclaw represents the cat's
life line, and the four claw pads represent
appetite, love, intelligence and luck,
from left to right when looking at the paw face up.

In the fourteenth century,
people were suspicious of cats
and they were suspected to be the familiars
of witches. Many cats were killed
in these unenlightened times.

One of the reasons that the Black Death
was as devastating as it was,
was because the lack of cats due to this
led to a rapid increase in the rat population.

Marijuana has been known to cause
fatal seizures in cats. How people

found this out, it's probably
best not to know.

A female cat is said to be spayed,
while a tom cat is neutered. A cat who has not had
either of these procedures is called 'whole'.

If a tom cat is missing one or more
of his canine teeth,
he cannot mate with a female.

This is because he will be unable to
effectively grab hold of his lady friend's
scruff at the back of her neck to effectively
manoeuvre himself without them.

A litter of cats can all have different fathers.
This is called superfecundation.

There is a morning after pill for cats.
It's called estrodiol cypionate and
can be administered up to 40 hours after mating.

Cats can also be pregnant
with two separate litters.
The queen may or may not
give birth to these at the same time.

CATNIP - THE FACTS

Other than driving moggies wild, catnip can also be used as an insect repellent. It's ten times more effective than DEET.

Although catnip grows in the wild, there are also catnip farms, where high-quality catnip is grown.

Location, climate and the type of soil all affect the quality of catnip.

The chemical that cats react to in catnip is called Nepetalactone.

Catnip plants need to reach a certain age before there is enough nepetalactone in them for cats to react to it.

The leaves, stems and flowers of the plant are all harvested as they all contain the chemical that makes cats go crazy.

Catnip belongs to the mint family. Fresh catnip that isn't 'mature' smells minty.

There are over 250 different varieties of catnip.

The Latin name for catnip is Nepeta Cataria.

Other names for catnip are catswort and catmint.

You can also make tea with catnip. It's said to be calming.

Fresh catnip leaves are also believed to be able to help heal cuts. Crush up a few leaves, add a splash of water and apply them to the cut to find out if it works or not.

Catnip causes cats' hearts to beat a little faster.

To keep it in tip top condition, it's best to keep catnip in a sealed container in the fridge.

Most cats in Australia are not susceptible to catnip.

Kittens under about three months old and senior cats are generally unaffected by catnip.

Even big pussycats like lions and tigers can be affected by catnip.

The first people realized that cats were susceptible to catnip were likely to be circus animal trainers, who discovered that it made lions more docile.

The response to catnip can last up to fifteen minutes.

Once a cat has had a catnip 'fix' it will take an hour or possibly even two before kitty will become susceptible to the nip fever again.

Different cats react in different ways to catnip.

Male cats are more likely to be susceptible to catnip than females.

Some cats will seem fascinated by catnip and smell and lick it. Others will rub up against it and seem to be 'high'.

Other cats have an even more extreme reaction and will rub their whole body into it, roll around and sometimes even leap up into the air in delight.

One cat can react extremely to catnip while her sister may not react at all.

The world's largest commercial producers of the catnip plant is a company called Cosmic Pet Products.

Kittens will always return to the same nipple to feed.

Although cats are typically weaned
by their fourth week,
some older cats will continue to suck on
their mother's teats long beyond that age.

Although kitten play may look brutal,
it is very rare
indeed for either of the kittens
to be injured by it.

A cat can kill its own prey from two months old.

Male cats seem to enjoy playing with toys
more than female cats do.

Love Crocs? They're dead classy, aren't they?
So I can understand why you might want a giant
Croc shoe bed for your kitty. You can order
them in a variety of different colours
from www.sasquatchpetbeds.com. You'd
have to persuade them to ship outside the US, though.

The longer a kitten stays with
his or her litter, the better
they will be at living with
other cats in later years.

If a mother cat is separated from
her litter for too long,
she will simply forget about them.

Likewise, former kittens who
are reunited with their
birth mother will not recognize her either.

Once about 50 days have passed, the mother cat
will consider her job to be done and leave her
kittens to their own devices from then on.

Generally, it seems even
neutered male cats will go
exploring outside - if given the chance - more
than spayed female cats.

You may have noticed some odd whiskers around
the house from where puss has shed them.
Some people like to collect and keep these.
If you don't have a
suitable container to keep them in, you can buy a
'Neko no Hige' – a wooden cat whisker
box – online from the Japan Trend Shop.

If you're thinking of adopting an older or
disabled cat, but cost is a concern, most shelters
will help pay the medical bill of such a
'special needs' cat.

You can use your cat's paw print as well
as your own fingerprint to unlock
the iPhone 5. Simply register kitty's paws

and no other puss will be able to use it to
order a takeaway pizza with extra tuna.

There is a species of cat called the
Jaguarundi that more closely resembles
a weasel than a feline.

Kittens need to eat approximately one and a
half times the protein of an older cat.
They're growing, you know!

Cats lose very little water through urination,
which is why cat urine smells so much more, uh,
concentrated than that of other animals.

This is also why cats noticeably
drink less water than humans.

Older cats can lose their sense of smell and taste,
which is why there is cat food
marketed at 'senior' cats.
It is smellier and tastier than regular
cat food to entice the older feline to have a nom.

If a cat is really, really hungry,
she will stop being fussy with her food.
Really.

Most cats won't eat pieces of kibble
that they've already nibbled on that have fallen
out of their mouths.

If you see the initials DSH or DLH on your
cat's vaccination book, these acronyms stand for
domestic short hair and domestic
long hair respectively.

The fluffy cheeks you see on some toms are
called 'stud jowls'. Toms that are neutered before
they reach sexual maturity won't have them.

You can tell if an older tom cat
was a bit of a ladies' man back in the day
by whether or not he has
these stud jowls. If he does,
he's likely to have lots of kittens
running around somewhere.

A cat uses her whiskers to measure whether
she can fit through a gap, however this won't work
if puss is too portly, which can lead to some
getting themselves stuck.

Cats generally can't chew kibble,
so they simply swallow it whole. The strong
digestive juices in their stomachs break it down.

When a cat (finally) wakes up, she will always give
her muscles a good stretch before attempting any
real exertion. First she'll arch her back
and then she'll stretch out her front then back legs.

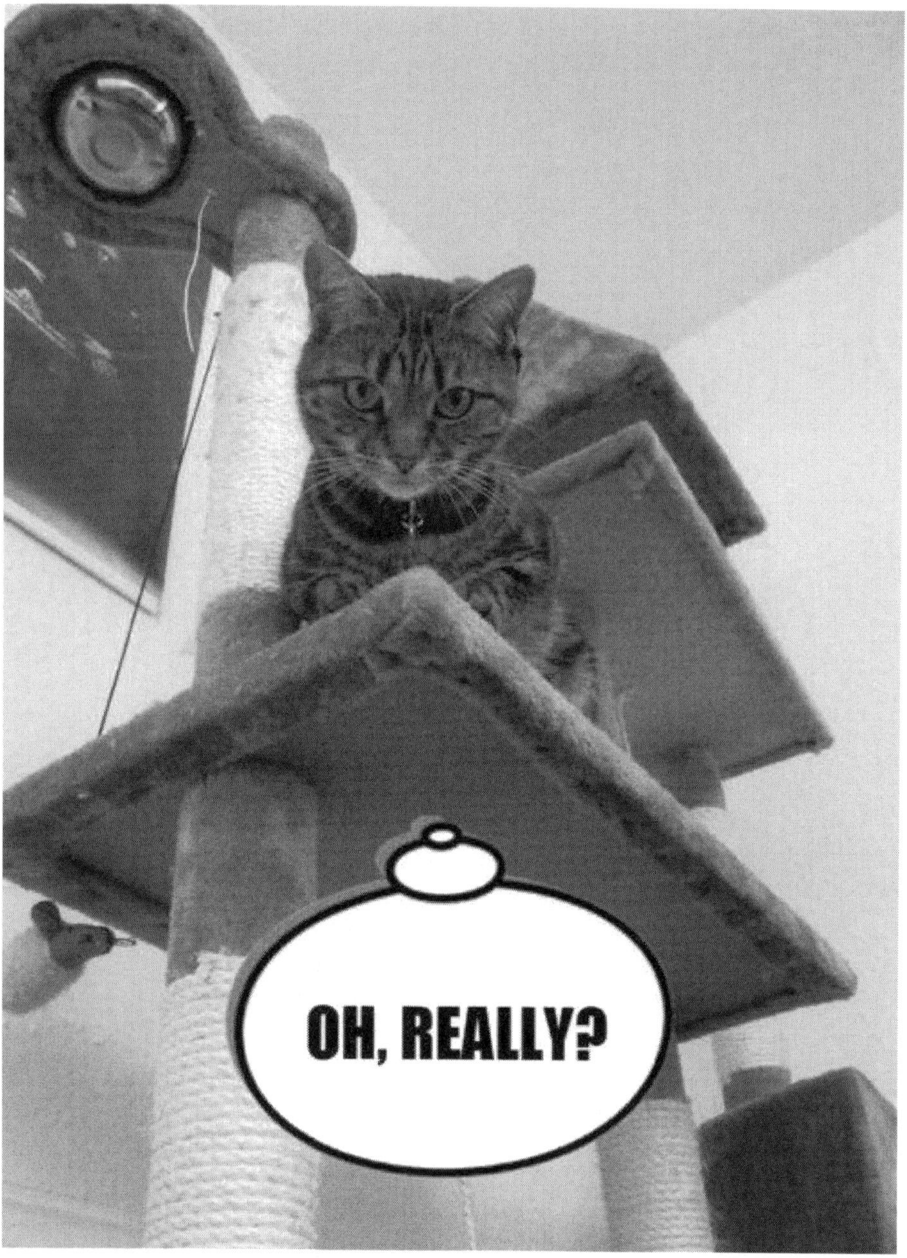
OH, REALLY?

Unless she is bought into a house with a littermate
as a kitten, most cats prefer to be the only cat in a house.

Even if a cat gets on with a sibling as a kitten, it's
no guarantee that they'll continue to get along
when they grow up.

The phrase 'the cat's pyjamas' comes from a
tailor who was said to make very fine silk
pyjamas. His name was E. B. Katz.

Ginger cats are can also be called
red, orange, yellow or marmalade.

Cats have less teeth than any other carnivore.

A Japanese study found that cats
hated rock music,
ignored muzak and quite enjoyed new age,
classical and instrumental tunes.

All Scottish Fold cats are related to
one single pussycat
called Susie, a white farm cat found
in Scotland in 1961,
who had a chance ear mutation.

There is a hearing aid for cats.
It was created by a German chap
called Hans-Rainer Kurz in 2003.

Cats' noses can be pink, orange or black.

Cats' paw pads will usually be all pink, brown
or black in colour. But some cats' paw pads
can be multicolour.

Cats can even have different coloured
paw pads on one paw. It's not unusual for a
black and white cat to have some
black paw pads and
some white, for example.

Some people refer to tabby cats
as 'the guys in the pinstripe suits'.

A typical cat blinks twice a minute.

A cat's claws are not their killing
weapons - they use
them to hold their prey still while
their teeth deliver
the killing bite to the
unfortunate victim's neck.

An easy way to tell the sex of a cat - if it's a male
the genitals will look like a colon.
If they're female they will look more
like an upside down exclamation mark.

The male's bits are also further
apart than the female's,
although it is notoriously hard to
sex young kittens, so
you may well not be 100 per cent sure.

If puss isn't being co-operative try stroking
the area above its tail. This will cause most
kittens to automatically raise their bottoms for
inspection and is known as 'elevator butt.'

A cat has scent glands on her paws,
along her back,
on the base of her tail,
on her forehead and on her lips.

Some cats' blood pressure can be seen to rise
when they pay a visit to the local vet.

Sixty-five per cent of cat owners give
puss a present at Christmas.

Twenty five per cent of cat owners celebrate
their pet's birthdays in some way.

A ginger tom cat called Spot
was probably the only cat
to ever be barred from the local pub - in fact,
he's been barred from all 50 of the local
pubs in his home town
of Hertford. His hard rocking owner
would bring him in
draped over his shoulders, but he was too
aggressive to the other punters.

Sphynx cats need to be kept indoors.

If you have more than one Sphynx cat, you should
be careful to regularly
trim each of their claws, or use
Soft Paws caps so they do real damage to each
other when they fight.

If you don't think that there are enough cats on
the Internet already, you should try Meowbify.
Key in a Web site's URL on the Meowbify site
and it will turn all the pictures into pictures of cats.

Littermates, if kept together, will often
remain fast friends for life.
Aside from that, the best chance
you have of your current cat(s)
accepting an addition
to the household is to bring in a kitten.

A chap called Edward Lowe
invented kitty litter in 1948.

Before that, pet cats either did their business
outside or in containers filled with sand or soil.

In the 1970s, clumping cat litter was created.

The most recent ancestor of the pet cat is believed
to be felis silvestris, the European wildcat.

This Latin name for the wildcat
is also the inspiration for the name
of the famous cartoon feline Sylvester.

The cat family is called the Felidae.

UNCONVENTIONAL USES FOR KITTY LITTER

When it's been snowing, kitty litter can make a good substitute for salt.

It can help provide traction for cars when placed on slippery roads.

Fill outside ashtrays with it so that smokers can bury their cigarette butts in it.

Pour a little into the bottom of a bin bag before using it so that it soaks up any liquid and also helps to keep the rubbish bag smelling sweet.

If you have musty old books that smell bad, try leaving them in a sealed container with some cat litter for a couple of days.

Put some cat litter in a sock, tie it up and place it inside a smelly shoe to get rid of those stinky stenches.

If you have a problem with moles in your back garden, pour some cat litter into one of their mole holes. They hate the smell and will find somewhere else to call home.

You can use cat litter to soak up spilled paint or oil. It's highly absorbent and an average sized bag of litter can soak up more than a gallon of paint.

Have a problem with a mouldy smelling sleeping bag or tent? Fill a sock with kitty litter, tie it up, chuck it inside and enjoy fresh smelling camping gear once more.

You can get rid of algae in your fish pond by adding a pound of cat litter to it for every 2,000 gallons of circulating water.

Put a shoebox full of cat litter into musty cupboards, basements or lofts to keep them from getting mouldy.

Having a barbeque? Cover the bottom of your grill with a thin layer of cat litter before you fire it up. The kitty litter will soak up the grease and help prevent it setting alight.

If your clothes have gotten wet from rain, the old kitty litter in a sock trick will help dry them out quickly.

Likewise, a sock full of kitty litter pushed inside the mouth of wet shoes will help them to dry out faster.

If you can bear it, you can use kitty litter to deodorize your fridge instead of baking soda.

You can use kitty litter to make dry flowers instead of using a press. Put a layer of kitty litter and the flowers in an airtight container, seal it and give it a week to work its magic.

If you mix soil with kitty litter when you're planting things in your garden, the litter will soak up moisture better than soil and keep your plants well watered.

Sprinkle cat litter on fresh oil spots on the road or in your driveway and leave for a few hours. Then sweep it up and dispose of it, along with the unsightly stain.

Many cigar aficionados use 100 per cent silica kitty litter inside their humidors to keep them working properly.

You can even use clay litter to make yourself a lovely face mask. Use a ratio of three tablespoons of cat litter to three tablespoons of water and grind it to a paste with a mortar and pestle. It's supposedly great for detoxifying the skin.

Cats are able to either roar or purr, but not both.

Polecats and Civet cats are not, in fact, cats.

The domestic cat is not actually the smallest cat in the world. A breed of wild cat called the kodkod from Chile is even smaller in stature.

In lion prides, there's something of a role reversal between the sexes. The females do all the hard hunting work, while the males just sit back and look pretty.

A cheetah is the only cat who has completely (back and front) non-retractable claws.

The tiger is the biggest big cat.

The puma is surely the cat with the most names - it is also sometimes called a cougar, mountain lion, panther, catamount, deer tiger and Mexican lion.

The Egyptian word for cat is - charmingly - Mau.

Ancient Egyptians mummified cats as well as humans.

In ancient Egypt, there were
two cat goddesses - Bast and Sekhmet.

Ancient Egyptians would shave their eyebrows off
as a sign of mourning when their cat died.

The oldest painting of a cat
dates to around 1950 BC and comes
from Egypt. It shows a cat crouching
under his mistresses chair.

No one really knows how cats made it to Europe
from Egypt, but it is believed it was via the Greeks.

The Ancient Greeks somehow managed
to keep their cats on leashes, like dogs.

The Romans kept both dogs and cats as pets.

Ancient Celts used to sacrifice cats.

Ancient Egyptians believed that cats
held the sun in their eyes after it set (no doubt due
to the way cats' eyes seem to glow at night)
and that they also could tell the future.

Lions and leopards
are the only cats mentioned in the Bible.

The Muslim prophet Mohammed,
was a big cat lover.
In fact, he had his very own cat,
a female tabby called Muezza.

Mohammed loved cats so much, he once
cut off his shirt sleeve when

his puss was resting on it,
so that he needn't wake her up to move.

A cat once saved Mohammed's life
from a poisonous serpent. As thanks,
Muhammad is said to have blessed cats so that
they would always land on their feet.

The two upward triangles on the
top of a tabby's face
are said to show the mark of
Muhammad's fingers as he affectionately
stroked the creature.

Not wanting to be outdone, Christians claim
this M marking on tabbies as their own, too.
Their story is that a cat
helped the baby Jesus drift off
to sleep by curling up next to him.
Mary was so grateful
she blessed the creature, who now sports
an M for Mary on its forehead forevermore.

An old Finnish myth does not have Death rowing
souls in a boat across the River Styx,
but in a sleigh drawn by cats instead.

The Vietnamese calendar is very similar to the
Chinese one except the rabbit animal is replaced
by the cat. Years of the cat include 1951, 1963,
1975, 1987, 1999, 2011 and 2023.

Many cats are fond of eating coconut.

Worried about dying alone a crazy old cat
lady (or man)? Don't worry, there's a dating site
specifically for you and other people who like cats.
www.purrsonals.com

Like Pinterest but think that there just aren't enough cats on it? You should try Catmoji, a Pinterest style online pinboard totally dedicated to cats.

In Japan, drunk tanks are called 'tiger boxes'. Rawr!

Back in the 1970s, coins from the Isle of Man would have the picture of the Queen's head on one side and pictures of different cats on the other.

Saint Francis of Assisi was very fond of cats, and so, during the thirteenth century, artists started to paint them in a more favourable light instead of as Satanic creatures.

The first image ever successfully transmitted on TV was of Felix the Cat.

Super capitalist Ayn Rand was a huge cat fan. She owned many kitties over the years, including cats named Junior, Turtle Cat, Thunderbird, Tartallia and Ali. She loved drawing pictures of her cats, wearing cat themed jewellery and once even revealed that she thought of herself as a cat.

Cats can make around 100 different sounds, whereas dogs only have 10 in their vocabulary.

A cat consumes an average of 127,750 calories each year, which is almost 28 times its own body weight.

Cats have a total of 13 ribs.

Cats intensely dislike the smell of citrus fruits
like lemons and oranges. Because of this,
sprays containing these make good training aids.

The first cat book ever written
was published in 1727.
It was written by French author
Francois-Augustin Paradis de Moncrif
and was called Les Chats.
The author was ridiculed
for the rest of his life for writing
a serious book on such a ridiculous,
un-scholarly topic.

Saint Gertrude is the Patron Saint of cats.

Cats with thin, wiry bodies
are more likely to be friendly,
vocal and territorial than those
with a stocky build.

Even completely domesticated cats are
accomplished hunters. When a pet cat goes after
a mouse, even if he has hunted before, he will be
successful once in every three attempts.

Cats walk on their toes, not their feet.

A cat can rotate her ears independently,
and round 180 degrees.

Cats have a total of 32 muscles that control
the precise movement of each ear.

A cat can fit through any
opening the size of its head or larger.

Don't ever try to have a staring contest
with a cat. Cats don't need to blink.

Cat urine glows under a black (ultraviolet) light.

25 per cent of cat owners say
that they blow dry their kitty's fur after a bath.

Some 900 vets in the US provide
acupuncture as a complementary therapy
for cats.

Americans spend more money per annum
on cat food than they do on baby food.
Cat food costs come to a grand total of four billion
dollars yearly, whereas baby food spending
only totals three billion.

You can buy wigs for your cat.
Really. Go to www.kittywigs.com if you
don't believe me.

The average cat owner spends around
£150 ($250) a year on cat boarding or
cat sitters while they play away.

Rarely, cats can be born with four ears.

Another mutation gives cats' ears a rounded
rather than pointed shape. This mutation
has been found in kitties in both
Italy and Texas.

Cats have been reported since 1890
as occasionally
being born with 'wings'.
They can't use these to fly,

they're more extra flaps of furry skin
that are a result of a skin disorder.

Shelters for unwanted pets were first
set up during the 19th Century.

According to British folklore, cats that are
born during the month of May are unlucky.

Cats' paw pads are, all at the same time,
both incredibly sensitive and extremely tough.

Feral cats often look dirty because they are
exposed to more muck than even the
most fastidiously clean cat can deal with.

In heavily populated urban areas,
up to 10 cats can time share an area.

A 'catio' is an enclosed outdoor area
for indoor cats to enjoy sunshine
and bird watching in safety.

Some official breeds of cats
have already disappeared,
including the Mexican Hairless
and the Chinese Lop.

New breeds are also being recognized all the
time, including the Lykoi and the Cuban Blue in 2010.

Albino cats are extremely rare, making up
only 2 per cent of all cats in total.

Albino cats have pale pink skin, white fur
and pinkish red or light blue eyes.
Most albino furries have blue eyes, making
the pink-eyed albinos very rare indeed.

In Belgium in 1879, some bright spark
had the idea of getting a team of 37 cats
together to deliver mail.
It didn't really work out.

In an average lifetime, a happy cat
will probably spend around 11,000 hours purring.

Mouse flavoured cat food WAS once considered,
but the tasting tester cats didn't think much of it,
so it was abandoned.

Most cats in Halifax (Nova Scotia) have six toes.

The word **MEOW** in various languages

Afrikaans: miauw
Albanian: mjaullin
Arabic: naoua
Armenian: meow
Belarusian: miau
Bulgarian: myaukane
Cantonese: mao
Catalan: meu
Chinese: miao
Croatian: mijau
Danish: miav or mjav
Dutch: miauw
Filipino: ngiyaw
Finnish: miau
French: miaou
German: miau
Greek: naiou
Haitian Creole: meo
Hebrew: miau and sometimes miya
Hindi: myau
Hungarian: miau
Icelandic: mja
Indonesian: meong
Italian: miao
Japanese: nyan, nya, n'yao or myah

Korean: yaong or nyaong
Lithuanian: miau
Malay: miau
Polish: miau
Romanian: miau
Russian: miau
Sanskrit: madj
Serbian: mijauuuu
Spanish/Portuguese: miau
Swedish/Norwegian: mjau
Turkish: mijav
Ukranian: niau
Vietnamese: meo-meo
Yiddish: myaw

Cats have a 220 degree field of vision.
Humans only have a 180 degree field.

The most common items for cats to steal
are gloves and shoes.

Five per cent of neutered females and
ten per cent of neutered males still spray.

The British Shorthair, Maine Coon and Bombay
are the easiest cat breeds to train.

There is a Web site called
www.catsthatlooklikehitler.com,
dedicated to…
yup, you guessed it.

A cat that has a Hitler-style
moustache is also sometimes referred to
as 'A Kitler'.

There's a productivity tool called Written? Kitten!
It rewards you for writing by displaying a new
picture of a kitten whenever you type 100 words.
writtenkitten.net

A cat's sense of smell is
14 times stronger than ours.

It's now believed that cats are actually NOT
colour-blind, and that they can see
blues, reds and greens.

Cats think of us as large cats,
not as themselves as small humans.

Male cats used to be called 'rams' or 'boars'.
When a book titled The Life and Times of a Cat
caught on, people started to call them Toms
instead, after the main character.

Cats have existed
longer on this planet than humans.

The domestic cat is the only type
of cat that can walk with its tail upright.

The life expectancy of cats
has nearly doubled in the last 50 years.

In multi-cat households, it's the members of the
opposite sex usually get along better.

A cat's heart beats at 110 to 140 beats
per minute, twice as fast as a human's.

In America, 37 per cent
of all homes have a cat.

Cats were originally brought
to the Americas to protect stores of grain.

Cats have been domesticated for
only half as long as dogs - and on their own terms.

Ragdolls are the biggest pet cats - females
weigh between 10 to 15 pounds
and males 12 to 20 pounds.
The smallest breed is the Singapura.

It is usually cat dander,
not cat hair that causes an allergic reaction in people.

Altruistic cats can be blood donors to other
kitties, if needed. Just like humans,
they'd need to be the right blood type, though.

Cats can be right brained or left brained,
with the opposite side of the brain
controlling the other part of the body.

In California, there is a cat holiday resort,
department store, a rent-a-cat agency, numerous
cat psychics, a cat dating service, cat shrinks,
acting coaches, a home for elderly cats
and the State also hosts an annual meowing contest.

Neutering a male cat will means he roams
less far away when he heads out the cat flap.

There are several pubs in England called
The Cat and Fiddle. There's one in between
Buxton & Macclesfield
(which is also, incidentally, the second tallest
pub in England), one in Christchurch,
one in Birmingham and many others.

Cats should not come into contact
with catnip until they are at least two months old.

Cats and dogs are not, in fact, natural enemies.
If they are brought up together as puppies
and kittens, they can be best friends.

Hairballs are the most common reason that cats vomit.

Sixty to eighty per cent of cats hack up
at least one hairball a month.

There are two types of hairballs.
One type forms in the
back of the throat and the
other in the stomach.

Cats can get acne, just like teenagers.
They can get spots
under their chins and
no one really knows the reason.

Cat bites are much more likely than dog bites
to become infected. Only 20 per cent of dog bites
compared to 40 per cent of cat bites go nasty.

The top selling cat toy is the Da Bird.
This comes heartily recommended from
this household, too!

At six months, a kitten is already approximately
the size she will be as an adult cat.

However, kittens can continue to grow until they
are up to two years old, or in the case of Maine
Coons, four years old.

There are over two million cat videos
on YouTube.

It is believed cats groom themselves so much
because keeping clean means their smell is
less strong and less likely to
alert prey to their presence.
Grooming also helps to keep cats cool.

Seven of the rarest breeds of cat
are the Khao Manee,
Napoleon, Donskoy, Minskin, Highlander,
Serengeti, and the Sokoke.

The first known use of the word LOLcat was
made on the 4chan message boards in 2005.
The site would feature cat photos every
Saturday – which it called Caturday.

However, the idea of taking silly photos of cats
is not exactly a new thing. Back in the 1870s
a chap called Harry Pointer took pictures of
cats posing standing on roller skates or
bicycles with captions like 'Happy New Year.'

It was in 2006 that the LOLcats
phenomenon really
took off. That was the year that the URL
LOLcats.com was registered and the first mega
viral video of cat antics
– called Cat Vs Dog – found
its way into people's inboxes worldwide.

Believed to be the first big online cat video,
Cat Vs Dog has, since 2006, had over 10 million views.

Cats won't eat all mice. For instance,
they don't like the taste of deer mice
and will very rarely eat them.

Nicolas Cage once took magic mushrooms
with his pet cat, Lewis.

Nicolas, for no doubt entirely legal purposes,
had been keeping some magic mushrooms
in his fridge (as you do). Lewis snuck in
when the door was open
and his back was turned and wolfed down some

of the forbidden fungi. Deciding it would be
rude to let him trip out alone,
Nicolas promptly polished off the rest.

The very first edition of Webster's dictionary
described cats as "deceitful animals that when
angered are extremely spiteful."
The author, Noah Webster, clearly did not like cats.

In Ambrose Bierce's The Devil's Dictionary,
a cat is described as "A soft, indestructible
automaton provided by nature to be kicked when
things go wrong in the domestic circle."

One of the words for a group
of wild cats is a Destruction.

Cats seem to dream when they sleep.
The same areas in their brains as human
are active while they sleep.

In cat worshiping ancient Egypt,
it was illegal to take a cat outside of the country.
Officials would even journey overseas
and seek out Egyptian cats
to pay to bring them back to their homeland.

In Hong Kong, you can buy a
Hello Kitty pot noodle
in supermarkets. It features Hello Kitty coloured
face pieces in the broth.

There is a Hello Kitty themed BDSM
room in a love hotel in Osaka, Japan.

A cat is more likely to survive a fall from
seven storeys than three. This is because

they have time to right themselves
and prepare for landing.

CAT SUPERSTITIONS

To see a white cat on the road is lucky. - American superstition

It is bad luck to see a white cat at night. - American superstition

If a cat washes behind its ears, it will rain. - English superstition

A strange black cat on your porch brings prosperity. - Scottish superstition

A cat sneezing is a good omen for everyone who hears it. - Italian superstition

A cat sleeping with all four paws tucked under means cold weather ahead. - English superstition

When moving to a new home, always put the cat through the window instead of the door, so that it will not leave. - American superstition

When you see a one-eyed cat, spit on your thumb, stamp it in the palm of your hand, and make a wish. The wish will come true. - American superstition

In the Netherlands, cats were not allowed in rooms where private family discussions were going on. The Dutch believed that cats would definitely spread gossips around the town. - Netherlands superstition

To reverse the bad luck curse of a black cat crossing your path, first walk in a circle, then go backward across the spot where it happened and count to 13.

Cats don't like food that's come
straight from the fridge. It's too cold for them.

It was the Vikings who brought the ginger cat
with them to the Scottish Hebrides.

Another name for a group of cats is a Glaring.

In Tokyo, cats have their own temple
called Go-To-Ku-Ji.
Cats are buried there and there are also
carved cat statues, sculptures and paintings.

Sixth century Greeks kept cats,
but only as pets. They preferred to use
ferrets to catch mice.

Cats are great observers.
They can learn to turn on lights,
open cupboards and use door handles
by watching how people do these things.

Morphine generally makes people feel relaxed.
Not cats. Given morphine, they
become completely manic.

MOST POPULAR CAT NAMES 1980s

Going back to the 1980s a poll of favourite cat names taken by the Anderson Animal Shelter in Elgin, Illinois, found these were the most popular back in the day...

1. Boots
2. Fluffy
3. Kitty
4. Muffin (or Muffy)
5. Patches
6. Princess
7. Samantha (or Sam)
8. Smokey
9. Tiger
10. Tom

Cat lovers will be pleased to learn that the
phrase 'no room to swing a cat'
likely doesn't refer to an actual cat,
but the cat o'nine tails whip.

It is believed that cats are less prone
to obesity than other animals as they are
solitary rather than pack hunters.
The fat cat rarely catches the mouse,
so therefore, they need to stay svelte.

Edgar Allen Poe often wrote with a cat sitting
on his shoulder and took his cat Catarina
everywhere with him.

In 1942 in New Zealand, cats were hired as workers
in post offices because rats kept eating the mail.

Cats seem to hugely prefer the company of adults
to children, probably largely because children
are noisy and move erratically.

Neutered female cats are the most likely
to bring home prey as 'presents' for their owners.

The Pussy Willow tree is so named
from a Polish legend.
In the legend, a mother cat was crying after
they fell into the river.
The willow tree felt sorry
for her and lowered its branches so that the
kittens could climb up on to them
and make it back to dry land.

Cats are used in Paraguay to hunt rattle snakes.

The Romans brought cats to Britain.

Feline sex has no foreplay and only
lasts on average between 5 and 10 seconds.

Male cats have barbs on their penis,
which probably explains why female cats
don't appear to enjoy the sex act very much
and male cats tend to run away
very fast when they're done.

No real research has been done in this area,
but it is believed that cats
are as at risk of lung cancer
from second hand cigarette
smoke as humans are.
Another good reason to quit.

Marijuana might be related to catnip, but it's
dangerous for kitties.
It can make them hallucinate,
have seizures and sometimes even die.
Don't get your cat high.

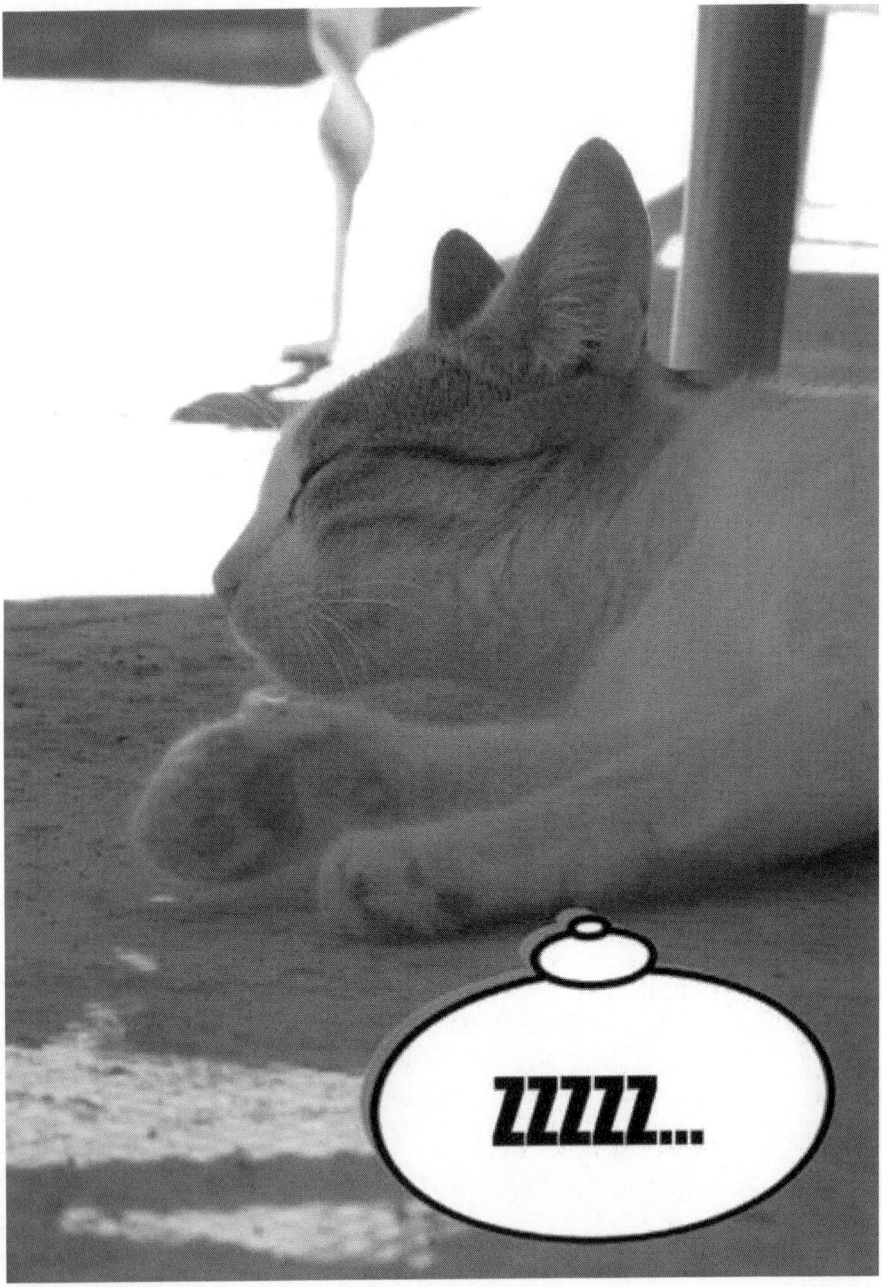
ZZZZZ...

A pub cat called Trixie from Wales seemed
to always be a bit under the weather.
After several trips
to the vet, her owners were still mystified
as to why until they realized that she was
sneaking up onto the bar
and drinking the beer from the overspill trays.
She wasn't sick. She was drunk.

Cats hate the smell of raw onions
being chopped and the odour
from all kinds of vinegar.

The top speed of 30mph that cats can reach
when they run is as fast as the top speed of the
white-tailed deer, the warthog and the grizzly bear.

Oriental cats like the Siamese are the most vocal.

When people talk on the phone, cats join in
because they think that person
must be talking to them.
There's no one else there, right?

Cats have a grooming routine - they start
by licking one of their paws to wash
the side of their face and finish up
licking the very tip of their tail.

The Mesa Theater and Club in Grand Junction,
Colorado has a resident cat called George Cat.
He can often be seen perched on a bar stool
eating his Fancy Feast with a shot glass of water
to wash it down.

One researcher has found that keeping pet cats
all your life adds about
10 years to your life expectancy.

A cat's vision is typically 20/100
compared with a human's 20/20.

It seems that cats can see faraway objects
extremely well, but closer items can become blurred.

An ultrasound can show kittens from
22 days after mum becomes pregnant.

A cat's claws grow in layers.
The outer layers shed every 4-6 weeks.

The singer-songwriter Cat Power changed her
name from Chan Marshall after seeing the words
'Cat Diesel Power' on a trucker's cap.

The Queen song Delilah was written
by Freddie Mercury in Switzerland about
one of his cats.

If you listen carefully to the lyrics, you'll
notice that one of the lines is, 'you make me so
happy when you cuddle up and
go to sleep beside me,
and then you make me slightly mad when you
pee all over my Chippendale suite.'
Brian May's guitar solo
part also features what
sounds like meowing noises.

Freddie also dedicated one of his entire solo
albums Mr Bad Guy to 'all the cat lovers
across the universe – screw everyone else.'

Only one of Freddie Mercury's many
cats – Tiffany –came from a pedigree breeder.
She was a Himalayan Blue Point.
The rest of his brood were rescue cats
from The Blue Cross.

Freddie owned nine kitties in total –
Tom, Jerry, Oscar,
Tiffany, Delilah, Goliath, Miko, Romeo and Lily.

Freddie Mercury missed his cats
terribly when he went on tour. He would
call home periodically to talk to them.

Whereas puppies need to be house-trained by
their human masters and mistresses,
a mother cat will show her kittens
how to use a litter box so we don't have to.

Cats are very territorial animals.

If a cat has diarrhoea, try giving her
scrambled eggs (make them
without adding milk
or butter, just literally scrambled eggs).
It can help bind the poo.

If a cat is peeing or pooping away from his
litter tray, be sure to rule out any
illness with a trip to the vet before
starting on trying to fix the problem.

Cats cannot chew their food.
Their teeth can only tear it.

Adult cats stand at around 8-10 inches tall.

From the tip of their nose to the tip of their tail,
a cat measures around 18-20 inches in length.

A cat's tail is around 10-15 inches long.

CAT COLOUR CODING

As far back as 1872, people have tried to claim that different coloured cats have different characteristics. I don't personally think there's anything in it, but it's fun to check them against your puss all the same.

CALICO
These kitties are said to be lovely and full of energy, as well as being lucky for both themselves and their owners.

GREY
Grey cats are sophisticated and slightly snooty. However, beneath the surface they really just want to go a little bit crazy.

GINGER
Sometimes called red, orange or ginger, these cats are supposed to have the sweetest nature of all the different colour varieties as well as being sassy and doing unpredictably hilarious things.

TABBY
These mini tigers are said to be good-natured and friendly and to enjoy relaxing even more than the average puss.

BLACK AND WHITE
This variety of cat is supposed to be the most independent and roam the furthest from home.

WHITE
An all white cat is said to be both irritable and clingy. This particular trait may actually have some truth in it, as many white cats are deaf and they also have a high chance of having poor vision and skin disorders. That's enough to make anyone grumpy!

BLACK
These poor pussies are always the last to get adopted from rescue centres, perhaps because of their reputation for being wilder and less predictable than other cats? Others describe them as both friendly and stubborn.

SEAL POINT
Seal point cats like Siamese have a well-deserved reputation for being attention seeking and extremely vocal. They are also said to form strong attachments to one person in particular and being extremely affectionate with them. For this reason, they tend to bond well with teenagers.

TORTOISESHELL
Poor tortoiseshells are another colour that may have an unfair reputation - they are known to be cheeky, mischievous and naughty. There's even a phrase for them - naughty torties.

CREAM, GREY, LILAC
These colours are said to be playful as well as curious and alert. They also are believed to need constant attention, which some owners may find annoying.

Apparently, there has steadily been an increase
in the number of 'alcoholic cats'.

Some cats seem to genuinely like the
taste of beer and actively seek it out.

Female cats weigh between 6-10 pounds.
Male cats weigh between 10-15 pounds.

Judas, the betrayer of Jesus, is often portrayed
in pictures with an evil looking pussycat by his side.

Leonardo Da Vinci seemed
somewhat fascinated by cats.
One of his sketch books contains
20 pencil pictures of
cats in various positions.

There have been seven cigars named after cats.
These were Two Toms, Cats, Old Tom,
Pussy, Tabby, Me-Ow and White Cat.

It is believed that the Havana Brown cat
was so named as the cat's coat
resembles the colour of a Cuban cigar.

Black Cat was a brand of cigarettes
that were introduced
into the UK in 1904 and the middle
of World War Two.
They were brought back again in 1957
for a couple of years and then in 1976 until 1993,
when they disappeared again,
this time probably for good.

Former US President Bill Clinton
famously kept a cat
called Socks at the White House
with him during
his presidency. He was very protective of her
and forbade photographers to touch her.

Less well known is that Bill Clinton is, in fact,
allergic to cats. He had to take shots
to keep his allergy to Socks under control.

RAF wing commander Guy Gibson flew during
World War Two with his cat, Windy,
in the cockpit with him.

A cat called Mourka from Stalingrad
carried messages
between Russian scouts and their home base.

Only two cats have ever been sent into space.

Until the 20th century, you are unlikely to see
a black cat in any American art. This is because
of a superstition that drawing one
would summon the unlucky creature into life.

Cats have been said to symbolize a whole range of
different things over the years.
Some of these things are
women, witches, Satan, evil,

fertility, independence,
the sun, vampires and magic.

Koko was a gorilla based at Stanford University
who was taught to communicate
with sign language.
When she was 12 years old,
she asked for a pet cat.
She was given one by her keepers
and called him All Ball.

When her pet cat, All Ball died,
Koko the Gorilla signed
'Bad, sad, bad' and 'Frown, cry, frown, sad.'

Later, Koko was allowed to pick
out two new kittens
from a litter to be her new companions.
She called them Lipstick and Smoky.

In the 1930s, when British health officials
banned the transporting of food on commercial
airline flights, cats were used to sniff out
any nosh that had been snuck in.

When cats walk, their back paws will end up
in exactly the same spots that their front paws
have just left. The same is true of foxes.

A cat's reflexes are faster than a dog's,
which probably explains why Rover very rarely
actually catches Tiddles, despite
his enthusiasm for the task at hand.

A cat that grooms excessively - to the point that
bald spots start appearing on her fur - is suffering
from a condition called psychogenic alopecia.

If there is no medical reason
for this over grooming,
it is common to prescribe Prozac for the cat.

The most common issue that animal behaviour
consultants report they hear from people
about their felines is litter box problems.

Other common cat problems are, in order,
aggressive behaviour, being a scaredy cat
and destruction of household objects.

A twitching tail means kitty is excited,
but a tail that's wagging back and
forth means she's angry.

When a cat drapes his tail around another cat
it's a sign of friendship, like putting an arm
around someone's shoulders.

Cats puff up their tails when they are frightened
to make themselves look bigger
and more intimidating.

The Korat cat is also known
as the 'Good Luck Cat of Thailand'.

The number one reason why cats are brought
to rescue centres is because the
owner has too many cats.

The three next most common reasons
are, in order, allergies, moving house
and the cost of keeping the cat.

HOW DO YOU MEOW?

Meow has many alternative spellings. Which do you prefer?

mieaou

maiou

maiow

meaow

meaw

meow

meow

mew

miaou

miaouw

miaow

miau

miauw

miaw

mieaou

miow

mi-owe

In Switzerland, if you are adopting a cat,
there is a law that states you have to adopt
at least two at a time, so that they can keep
each other company.

The younger the cat, the
softer the fur.

Female cats are in general, less welcoming of new cats.

One line of wisdom is that, if you have an
adult female as your only cat,
a female kitten will make the best match.
A young, active male would
appreciate another of the
same. An older male cat will be happy
with a kitten of either sex.

In 2005, Mischief, a cat from Stevenage,
was named Pet Slimmer of the Year after
he lost 11 kilos in nine months.

Most cats aged between one and four years old
will happily self regulate how much they eat,
meaning you can leave food

out for them all the time
so they can graze whenever they like.

Never use a flea product that
has been designed for
dogs on cats. Some of these are extremely toxic
to kitties, and puss can even die.

The most important thing you can do to help
your cat's teeth healthy is feed her crunchy things.

If kitty's breath smells, it's likely he has
gum disease or an infected tooth.

The most likely reason that a cat
won't use a litter box
is that it is too dirty or smelly. Don't forget,
cats have a much keener
sense of smell than we do.

Other common reasons for litter box problems
are - in order - there aren't enough litter boxes,
the cat doesn't like the litter and the cat
has been stressed out by something like moving
house or a new cat in the house.

You should have one litter box for every cat
in the household. Some people even believe you
should have one more litter box than
you have cats, just to be sure.

Cats are not spiteful -
they will never wee somewhere
or do something 'bad' to punish you.
They just don't think like that.
Don't make the mistake of
projecting human behaviours on to them.

Urinary tract infections like cystitis
should be ruled
out when troubleshooting litter box
problems, too.

Declawing cats makes them more likely
to have litter box issues, as the litter can
hurt their declawed paws.

Declawing is a controversial operation
that is performed
by some vets in the US
that removes the distal phalanges
of all toes on the front paws,
so kitty can no longer
scratch humans or cause
damage to their furniture.

The 'proper' name for declawing is an onychectomy.

Declawing is illegal in the UK,
and many other countries.

When Buddhism came to Japan, it was customary
to have at least two cats in the temple
to protect the manuscripts from mice.

Cats were the only live animals allowed
inside ancient Roman temples.

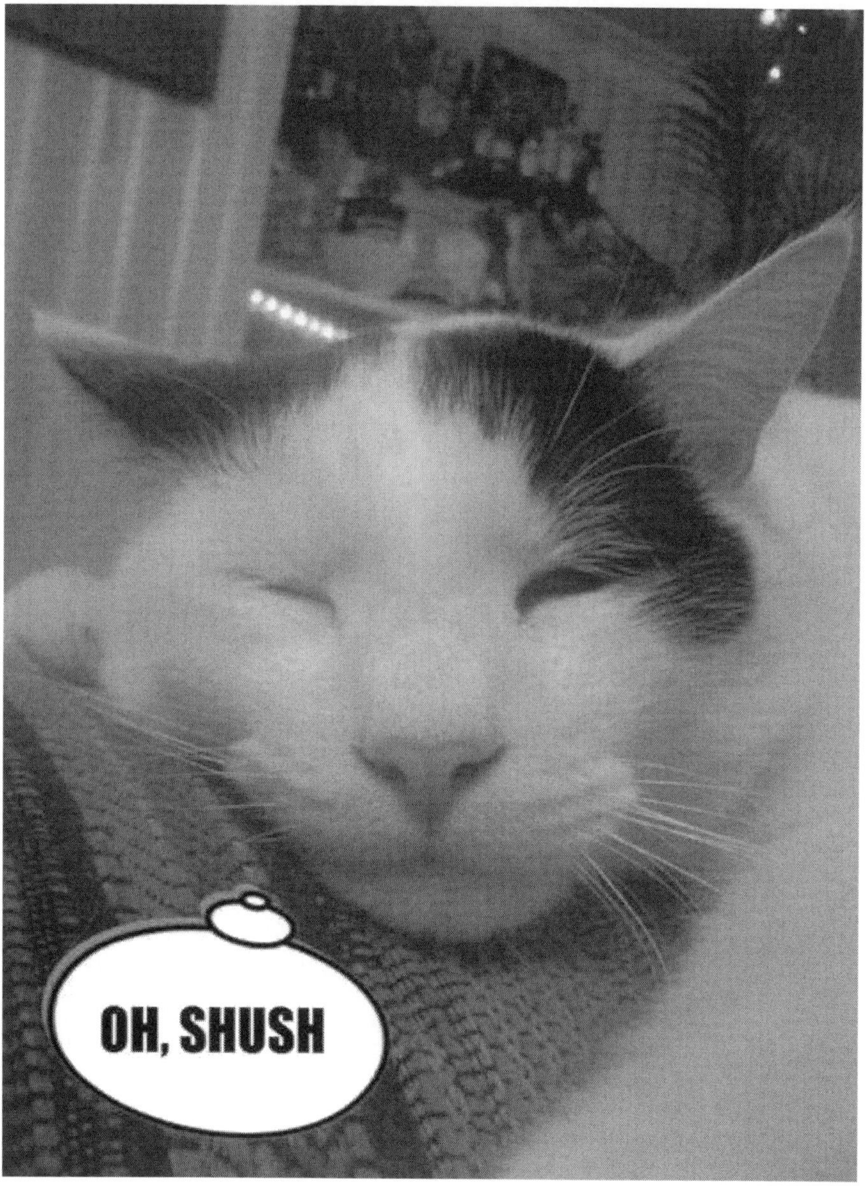
OH, SHUSH

The small door made in Spanish houses for cats
to get in and out is called a gatera.

Although it may be difficult to believe,
a cat's brain and a human's brain
are very similar.
They both have identical areas
responsible for emotion.

When a cat's tail quivers,
that's the biggest sign of love that
she can ever give you.

When a cat slow blinks at you,
you should slow blink
back. She's telling you she loves you and wants
to know that you love her, too.

A cat's vision is sharpest a few feet
from his face.

The most popular pedigree cat is the Persian,
followed by the Maine Coon and then the Siamese.

The Egyptian Mau is probably
the oldest breed of domestic cat.

If she has enough water, a cat can tolerate
temperatures up to 133 F.

In contrast to dogs,
cats have remained remarkably
uniform in size across all their different
breeds since domestication.

A falling cat can usually right itself in mid air
automatically. She will arch her back
to spread the impact of landing.

The way kittens are treated by humans
in the first few weeks of their lives
helps shape their personality.

Seven per cent of cats snore.

Cats lose almost as much liquid
from their bodies through
their grooming sessions
as they do through passing urine.

If a cat bites you, it is not always
a sign of aggression.
Cats will gently bite as a sign of affection
and it will tickle rather than break the skin.

Cats struggle to retain their body temperature
when they're wet.

When a kitty is scared, all the fur on her body
will stand up. But when she is angry,
only a narrow band of fur on her spine will.

The fur that grows out of a kitty's ears
is called 'ear furnishings'.

Ear furnishings help keep foreign objects
out of the ear and insulate them against the cold.

It is believed that a cat can hear her owner's
footsteps returning home
from hundreds of feet away.

The Turkish Van cat's coat
has a unique texture that
repels water, which is probably why,
unlike most other cats,
they seem to really enjoy going swimming.

The House of Mouse, Disneyland,
isn't so friendly towards actual mice.
They employ feral cats as mousers
to keep real rodents out.

At night after it's closed to the public,
Disneyland becomes overrun by the feral cats.
They're fed and looked after by the staff
in return for their mouse catching duties.

Another place that still employs cats as mousers
today is the State Hermitage
Museum in Moscow, Russia.

In the UK, although it is illegal to not report a
car accident involving a farm animal or a dog,
there's currently no legal recourse
if you fail to report hitting a cat.

A cat's kidneys are so efficient
that she can drink
sea water and filter it so
that it provides her with all the
rehydration she needs.

WORLD RECORD CATS

Smallest Cat
Mr. Peebles - born in 2005 - is the world's smallest cat, measuring just 6.1 inches tall. The itty bitty kitty is owned by Robert Svendson, who lives in Illinois, and was named after a ventriloquist's dummy that appears in the sitcom Seinfeld. Mr. Peebles weighs only 3.3lbs and is about the size of a guinea pig. The tabby cat's small stature is due to a birth defect.

Lightest Cat
The appropriately named Tinker Toy (a boy!) weighed only 820 grams. He was a tiny Blue Point Himalayan/Persian and lived for almost seven years, dying in 1997. He measured only 7 cm (2.75 inches) tall, and 19 cm (7.5 inches) long. He was born on Christmas Day 1990 and was owned by Katrina and Scott Forbes from Taylorville, Illinois.

Longest Cat
Stewart 'Stewie' Gilligan, a maine coon, had a body of 48.5 inches long. He was owned by Robert Hendrickson and lived in Reno. As well as being a world record holder, he also worked as a therapy cat.

Tallest Cat
Not entirely sure what the difference is between tallest and longest (I would have thought they were the same thing,

surely?) but Savannah Islands Trouble (Trouble for short) wins the tallest cat award at 19 inches tall when she was measured at the Silver Cats Cat Show in Reno, Nevada on October 30, 2011.

Longest Tail
Stewart 'Stewie' Gilligan also wins the Longest Tail world record, with his tail measuring 16.34 inches long. Sadly, Stewie died, aged eight from cancer, in February 2013.

Loudest Purr By A Domestic Cat
Smokey, owned by Lucinda Ruth Adams from Northampton in the UK, is the proudest owner of the loudest purr. Clocking in at 67.7 dB, Smokey achieved his world record at home, and according to the Guinness World Records web site "accessories used during the record attempt included a grooming brush, slices of ham and stroking by hand."

Most Kittens From One Mother
This slightly dubious honour belongs to Daisy, a Bonham, Texas-based feline, who was born in 1935. She gave birth to a massive 420 kittens during her lifetime, with her last litter on 12 June 1952.

Oldest Domestic Feline Mum
The unimaginatively named 'Kitty' is the world's oldest known domestic cat Mum. She gave birth at the grand old age of 30 to two kittens. Kitty died at age 32, having left behind 218 known descendants.

Longest Cat Whisker
The longest single cat whisker belongs to Missi, a Maine Coon who lives with her owner Kaija Kyllonen from Finland. The whisker in question measures 19 cm (7.5 inches). Missi's complete name is almost as long - 'Fullmoon's Miss American Pie' to be complete, and she was born in 2001.

Largest Domestic Litter
The average litter for cats is anywhere between one and six kittens, but larger litters are possible. The biggest on record was

19 kittens (sadly four were stillborn) on 7 August 1970 from a Burmese/Siamese mix puss called Tarawood Antigone belonging to a V. Gane of Oxfordshire in the UK.

Oldest Ever Cat
The oldest feline on record is Creme Puff, who lived for an astounding 38 years and 3 days. She was born on 3 August 1967 and died on 6 August 2005. Her owner, Jake Perry from Austin, Texas, was also the previous record holder for another cat, called Grandpa Rex Allen, who was 34 years and 2 months when he passed.

Richest Cat
The richest cat in the world is an Italian cat called Tommasino, who inherited almost £10 million when his owner died. His owner, Maria Assunta, had no living relatives when she died aged 94 in November 2009. The lukcy kitty is now the proud owner of several villas across Italy along with various bank accounts, stocks and shares. Tommasino beats the previous puss off the rich list – Blackie, who was left £9 million by his reclusive British owner in 1998.

Fattest Cat
The Guinness World Records has stopped accepting entries for this category as the team were concerned it was encouraging people to 'fatten up' their animals to unhealthy levels in an attempt to secure a place in the World Record Book and their fifteen minutes of fame. So, there's no telling whether this feline is still the official world's largest, but he was certainly a fat cat all the same. Himmy from Australia weighed in at 21.3kg (3st 4lbs) was the last recorded Guinness Record winner.

Most Toes On A Cat
A cat with more than five toes on her front paws or four on her back is called a polydactyl cat. This condition is not life threatening and doesn't affect the cat in any real way – for some unknown reason, polydactyl cats seem to be most common in clusters along the East coast of North America and in Wales and South West England. The current Guinness World Record

holder (since 2002) is Jake, who has a total of 28 toes and comes from Ontario in Canada.

Most Money Paid For A Cat
The most money spent on record for buying a cat is $41,435, which was spent in 1998 on an F2 Bengali kitty called Cato. She cost almost double the previous record holder, a Californian Spangled cat, that set its anonymous movie star buyer back $24,000 (£15,925) in 1987.

Most Expensive Cat Breed
Pedigree cats can be expensive, as anyone who's bought one will know. But while you're likely to pay a few hundred pounds for a genuinely pure puss, the most expensive cat breed will set you back considerably more than that. The Ashera is currently the most ridiculously dear cat, with each one costing approximately £10,796 (plus shipping). The breed was created by British businessman Simon Brodie, who created the genetic cross breed in a US lab. The Ashera cat will grow to over a metre tall with a top weight of 30lb and is a mix of the African serval, the Asian leopard cat and a domestic puss.

Oldest Janus Cat
A Janus Cat is otherwise known as a 'two-faced cat', but that doesn't mean she's saying nasty things behind your back – she's literally a cat with two faces combined, a little like human Siamese twins. Named after the Roman god with two faces, the longest living Janus cat is called Frank and Louie, who come from Massachussetts and reached 12 years old in September 2011. The average life expectancy of a Janus cat is only one to four days, due to all the related health problems that come with having two faces. His owner, Marty, told a local radio station that the cat acts more like a dog as he, "walks on a leash and loves car rides."

Most Cats Owned By One Person
Think you've got a lot of cats? Think again. The most cats ever owned by one person is a staggering 689. This record is owned by proud cat man Jack Wright of Kingston, Ohio. He

commented, "You don't set out to do something like this. You can visualise a hundred cats. Beyond that, you can't." He's probably right.

Highest A Cat Has Fallen And Survived
While it's true that a cat automatically rights itself while it is falling for a better chance of surviving falls, it's inadvisable to push puss out of a high storey building to test the theory. The highest a cat has been recorded to have fallen and survived is from the sixteenth floor. The cat in question is called Andy and he belonged to Florida Senator Ken Myer. He fell from the window of an apartment building in 1973.

Most Flights By A Cat
It's generally unusual to see people flying with their pets when going on holiday, but a ginger cat called Smarty wasn't going to be left behind. Her owners often took her to Larnaca, Cyprus with them from their home in Cairo, Egypt and she clocked up some 80 confirmed flights. Her British born owners, Peter and Carole Godfrey say she made it to 97 flights before her death in 2007.

First Cloned Cat
The first successfully cloned cat was born in December 2001 at A & M University in Texas. The kitten was a white/tabby mix and named CopyCat (CC for short). She was the only one of 87 cloned kitten embryos to survive. In 2006, CopyCat gave birth to a litter of three kittens, all conceived naturally, and she's said to be happy and healthy.

Most Expensive Cat Wedding
Given that cats generally don't get married, this is likely to be Phet and Ploy, two cats from Thailand that tied the knot in 1996 in matching pink outfits. The wedding cost an estimated $17,000 (with an added dowry of $23,000) and included the groom (Phet) arriving in a Rolls Royce, while the bride (Ploy) flew in by helicopter. A parrot was the best man and an iguana agreed to be maid of honour. More than 500 people attended the ceremony. The cats both have sparkling diamond eyes,

considered to be lucky, but are in fact actually a sign of glaucoma.

A Savannah cat is a domestic cat crossed
with a wild cat called a Serval.
Some people believe
that Savannah cats act more like dogs than cats.
They are happy to walk on a harness,
follow their owners around and play fetch.

Savannah cats are banned in Australia.

Savannah cats are given classifications
like F1 – the F stands for Filial
and the number lets you know how
many generations away from a wild cat she is.
An F1 has a Serval cat as a parent, an F2 has
a Serval grandparent and so on.

The cat that Vito Corleone
strokes in the Godfather
was not in the actual script.
It was a stray that wandered on to the set.

One of the reasons that cats
can sometimes survive
falls from very high places
is that they have a much
lower terminal velocity than humans.

Humans can fall at more than 120mph
whereas cats only reach 60mph.

There are very few true black cats.
Most black cats will, on close examination,
have a small white patch or strands of white fur
somewhere on their bodies.

Most cats prefer to get their water and food
in separate places.
Going back to their time in the wild,
if a dead animal (food) is
located near to water,
it may mean the water is contaminated.
One of the reasons that cats will seek
out an alternative source of
water – from a toilet, perhaps? - is that
their food and water bowls are placed together.

The pouch of skin under a cat's stomach
is there because it gives them extra room
to stretch out when they run.

Black cats are the least likely to be adopted.
Rescue centres are almost always
full of black cats.

One third of cat owners believe
that their cat can telepathically read their mind.

The growth hormone
is only released in kittens
while they are sleeping,
which is probably the reason
why kittens seem to sleep so much.

The annual cost of keeping
a cat is half that of keeping a dog.

Although black cats tend to be thought
of as lucky in the UK, in the US
they are considered unlucky.

In the US, white cats are considered lucky.
If you find a white cat sitting beside
your front door and you are
going to get married soon,
the marriage will be filled with happiness.

President Lincoln kept four cats
during his time at the White House.

When Nikola Telsa received a static shock from
stroking his cat, it inspired him
to find out more how electricity worked.

A study found that cats CAN recognize
the sound of their owner's voice.
They just don't necessarily
choose to do anything about it.

Although cats in the UK and US are said to
have nine lives, in
Germany and Southern Europe,
they only have seven. In Arab countries,
this goes down even further to just six.

A ship called the RMS Empress of Ireland had a
resident cat called Emmy. She travelled
everywhere on the ship until May 28, 1914,
when she refused to get on board. The ship sailed
without her and sank the next day.

The RAF parachuted cats into Borneo
to clear up a serious rat outbreak in the 1950s.

MOST POPULAR CAT NAMES 1990

A Gallup poll in 1990 show that some things change while others stay much the same. The top 10 cat names for that year are as follows...

1. Baby
2. Blackie
3. Samantha
4. Tom
5. Tiger
6. Casper
7. Sylvester
8. Whiskers
9. Fraidy
10. Scardey

The lion is the only species of cat that lives
and hunts in a group - this is
called a pride rather than a pack.

Cats will almost never meow at another cat.
It's a sound they reserve for
communicating with humans.

Cats may react violently to being touched
on the belly as this is their most vulnerable place.

When a cat exposes his belly to you, he doesn't
necessarily want it to be touched. He's just
showing you that he feels happy and comfortable.

Most cats like being rubbed under the chin,
behind the ears, on the head
and at the base of their tail.

Some of the names cat owners have come up
with for their cats kneading are making biscuits,
mooshie feet, mashing potatoes, pummelling,
stomping grapes, furry bliss,
playing the piano and happy feet.

The tails of wild cats never rise
higher than their backs.

The total cat population of the world is
estimated to currently be at around 200 million.

In the US, there is one cat for every four people.
Here in the UK, the ratio is
about one cat for every ten
people. Unbelievably, in Austria,
there are the same amount of cats as people.

A small, short cat with a round face
is said to be cobby shaped.

A cat that is slender and has a narrow face
is said to be wedge shaped.

Siamese cats are said to be colour pointed
as they have colour only on their ears, face, paws
and tail. However, other breeds can
be colour pointed as well.

Blue cats like the Korat, Devon Rex
and British Blue Short Hair are actually grey.

There have been lots of scare stories in
the papers about the disease toxoplasmosis,
but in order to catch it, you would have to literally
touch cat feces and then touch an
open wound on your body.

And, even if you did do that, it would have to be
on one of the seven to ten days that the cat
had an active infection in her entire lifetime.

In fact, most human cases of toxoplasmosis
come from eating undercooked meat
and have nothing to do with cats.

People with pets are most likely to travel
with their dogs
(78 per cent of all travellers with pets).
Cats come in second but with
only 15 per cent of the total.

People tend to stick with the type of animals
they were raised with.
Therefore, if your family had
a cat while you were growing up, you're more
likely to keep a cat yourself in later years.

Cats that live closer together than they would like
will tend to 'time share' territory,
going outside at different times of the day.

Between two and seven weeks old is the most important time
for a kitten's social development.

Trauma can change a cat's personality.

After a cat has recovered from a traumatic event
like a car accident, she goes through a second
socialization process, similar to the one
she went through as a kitten.

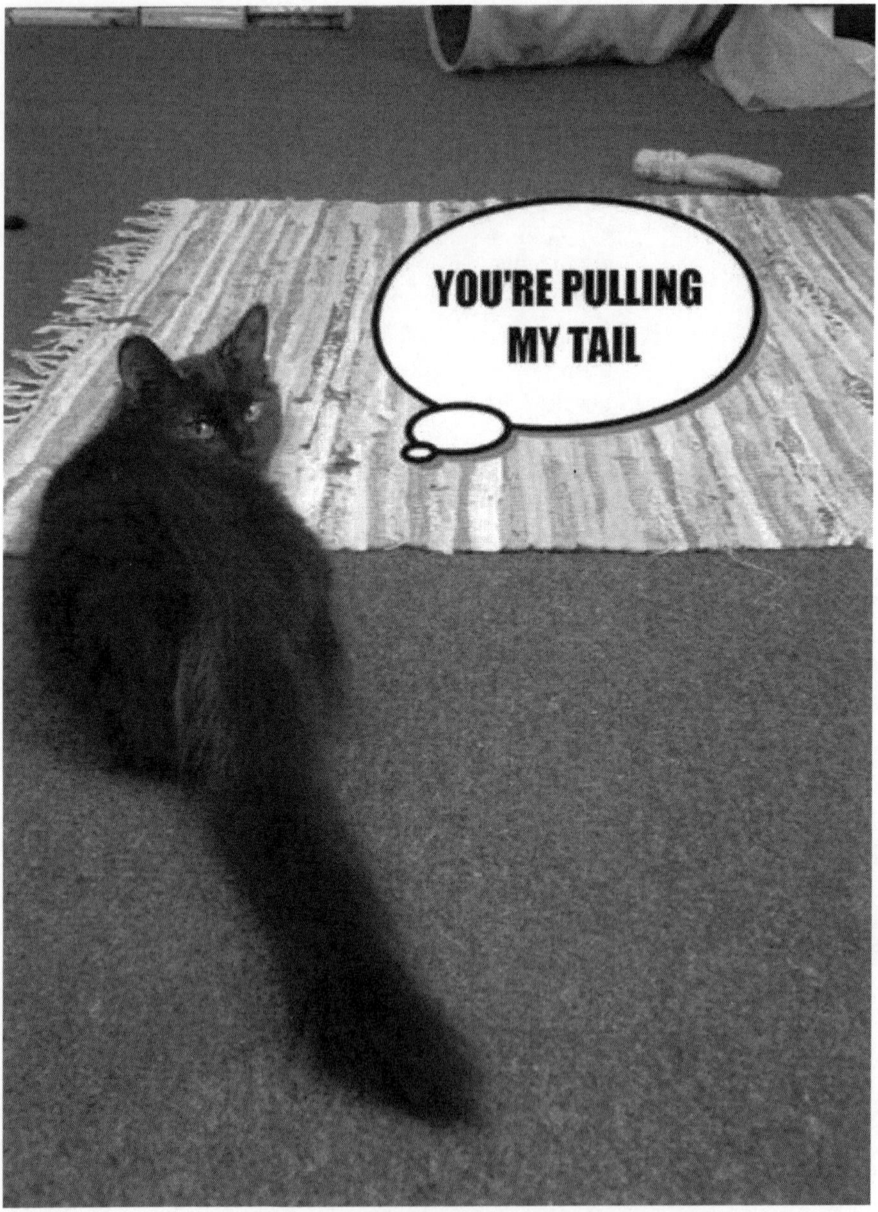
YOU'RE PULLING
MY TAIL

After the second socialization process,
the cat can become more sociable
or more withdrawn.

When a cat rubs against another cat,
he's mingling their scents together
to show that they're friends.

Cats who are friends
will touch noses to greet each other.

Nose to nose greetings confirm the
cat's identities and also allow them
to check how the other cat is doing,
where she has been and what they've been up to.

Cats find it hard to judge our moods
because we don't have tails.

Cat's eyes can be coloured green, gold, blue or copper.

The part of a cat's eyes that seems to glow
in the dark is called the tapetum lucidum.

The tapetum lucidum is also present in the eyes
of dogs, some fish and birds and many
other nocturnal creatures.

Cats have been used as spies because
they have such an acute sense of
smell and very sharp hearing

Project Acoustic Kitty was a secret CIA
project launched in the 1960s which cost some
$25 million and was intended to use cats
to spy on the Russians by implanting electronic
transceiver equipment inside the animals.

Project Acoustic Kitty
was abandoned in 1967 as a failure.

Fred the Undercover Kitty was a tabby cat
who worked for the New York Police Department.
He was brought in as an undercover agent
in a sting to arrest a man
working as a vet without the proper credentials.

Cats use an especially annoying purr
when they want something in order
to manipulate us into giving in.

Oscar, a cat who lives in a care home in
Providence, Rhode Island,
can predict a patient's death.
If he sits with a resident,
they tend to die very soon after.

Believe it or not, some cats enjoy going to the vets.
In fact, some cats purr so loudly when they're there
that it's impossible to hear their heartbeat
through the stethoscope.

Research suggests that the sound of purring
could help wounds to heal and bones
to knit back together.

Purple is the most eye catching colour to felines.

Cats have true fur -
that means that they have both
an undercoat and over coat of fluffiness.

There is a Hawaiian band called Cringer, which is
named after a talking cat from the cartoon He-Man.

The German word Katzenjammer
(also the surname
of Fran in Black Books) means literally
'cat's wall' and
translates as 'discordant sound'
or 'the blues'. Germans
sometimes use it to describe a hangover.

A portion of cat food contains the
nutritional equivalent of about five mice.

A male cat can only have orange
or black in his coat, not both.
However, female cats
can have a combination of the two.

In the rare case that a male cat does have both
orange and black in his coat,
he is almost always sterile.

Siamese kittens are born completely white
and develop their other colourings as they grow up.

One rescue centre worker reports
that among the stupid
names that cats who have been
brought in have been
called are Bong, Douchebag, Lil' Hitler, Rabid,
Dick, Al Qaeda, Slutbutt, Pissy, Redneck and…
Tabby Turdstockings.

Cats can be taught to walk on a leash or harness,
but generally only if you start
walking them on it when they are kittens.

Some cats are horizontal scratchers
and some are vertical scratchers.

It is thought that tabby cats take their name
from a district in Baghdad called Attab.

A cat laps up water with its tongue backwards.

According to a series of tests undertaken
by the Department of the American Museum
of Natural History, a dog's memory lasts about
five minutes whereas a cat's can last up to 16 hours.

Tom cats are always ready to mate,
but females have to be on heat.

Dominant cats purr when they approach
cats that are lower down the food chain.

Cats can also purr when
they're sick to let other cats
know they're not feeling up to play fighting.

Fish bones are the most dangerous to cats.

Most cats prefer eating fish to eating meat.

The most expensive time to
buy a kitten is just before Christmas.

CRAZY CAT LAWS

In French Lick Springs, Indiana, there was once a law requiring all black cats to wear bells on their collars on Friday the 13ths.

In Lorinc, Hungary in 2001, a new law was passed stating that cats could only be allowed outside on a lead. This was to save the public from the "dangerous menace of free range cats."

In International Falls, Minnesota, cats are not allowed to chase dogs up telephone poles.

In Barber, North Carolina, dogs and cats are forbidden from fighting by law.

In Sterling, Colorado, a pet cat is not allowed to roam free without a tail light.

In Ventura, California, cats must have a permit before having sex.

In Cresskill, New Jersey, cats are required to wear not one but three bells on their collars in an effort to protect local birds.

In Duluth, Minnesota cats are not allowed to sleep in a bakery.

In Zion, Illinois you are not allowed to give your cat a lit cigar to smoke. Even if she asks nicely.

In Columbus, Georgia, cats are forbidden to yowl after 9pm.

In Topeka, Kansas, you are not allowed to have more than five cats at any one time.

In Shorewood, Wisconsin, this is limited even further - one family is not allowed to keep more than two cats at a time.

In Virginia, a state wide law bans dogcatchers from 'bothering' cats whilst they are going about their work.

In Reed City, Michigan you are not allowed to own both a pet cat and a pet bird.

In Philadelphia, cats are required to wear seatbelts (presumably around their carriers). If they don't, they are subject to a hefty fine.

In California, cats are not allowed to have sex within 1,500 feet of a tavern, school or place of worship.

In Montgomery County, Maryland they passed a law in 1999 that prohibits cats from visiting another person's property. Fines start at $100 for non compliance.

In Baltimore, Maryland, it is illegal to take a lion to the movies.

Many rescue centres don't allow adoptions in
the run up to Christmas as they want to avoid
people giving kitties to kiddies as presents.

In the US, if you can persuade a store that you're
going to be eating the cat food
you're buying yourself,
then it will cost less.
That's because there's no sales tax
on human food, but there is on pet food.

Cats don't have any of the taboos
that we humans have.
That means, if you don't neuter them,
Fluffy will have no problem mating with her
brothers, father or even sons.

A desperate cat may come on to a dog
if another feline isn't nearby.

Getting milk from their mother is
hard work for a tiny little kitten.

If your cat seems to meow but you can't hear
anything, it's probably because the meow
is simply out of the human range of hearing.

Cats can sometimes be attracted to the scent
of strange things like cosmetics, moisturiser
and shampoo because they contain animal products.

A survey found that most cat owners thought
that their cat gave them more affection than
their significant other.

If your cat is attacking you
for seemingly no reason,
it may be your perfume or aftershave.
Some of these contain scents
that come from wild animals.

If you suspect your cat might have fleas, look
at the skin below your knees.
If there are bites there,
your suspicions are likely well founded. This is
apparently fleas' favourite nibbling spot.

Flea collars don't work. Electronic flea collars
don't work at all, and regular flea collars
only work for a very short time.

Cats can overreact to stimuli because
they have something of an
overly sensitive nervous system.

If you travel with your
kitten in a carrier in your car,
he will likely get used to travelling
and be less likely to be
distressed by it in his later years.

Cats can get asthma.

It's true that cats will start to
frantically lick themselves

before a storm. No one knows why for sure,
but it's believed to be something to do with
the build-up of static electricity in the air.

Generally, the smellier cat food smells,
the more cats will like it.

The number one enemy of cats is cars.

When people were asked whether they would
rather have their significant other or their cat
with them on a desert island,
the answers were almost 50/50.

The cat's brain is so busy that more than
twenty per cent of blood pumped around the body
by the heart is directed straight there.

The name of the earliest cat on record is Bouhaki,
who is mentioned in Ancient Egyptian writings
that date back to 2000 BC.

In some cultures, calico cats are considered to be lucky.
In the US, they are sometimes called 'money cats'.

The Japanese Maneki Neko is almost always a calico cat.

If a Maneki Neko cat has her left paw raised,
that symbolises money is coming. If her right paw
is raised, it means good fortune is on its way.
Some even have both raised, which seems to me
to be a bit greedy.

In 1995, a green kitten was found in Denmark.
At first, it seemed as if the unusual colour
had been caused by a genetic mutation,
but it was eventually discovered to be caused by
a high copper content in the local water.

Putting a bell on a cat's collar may actually
make her into a better hunter. That is because
cats learn how to move without their bells ringing
and become even more stealthy
in their prey killing ways.

Although cats are accomplished sleepers,
bats and opossums beat them in the
snoozing stakes - they spend an average of
20 hours each day asleep.

There are actually three different types of
cat eye shapes - almond, round and slanted.

A cat's whiskers are two to three times
thicker than the rest of her fur.

Whiskers are rooted much deeper than the rest
of a cat's fur, too.
They are embedded about three times
as far as the rest of her fluff.

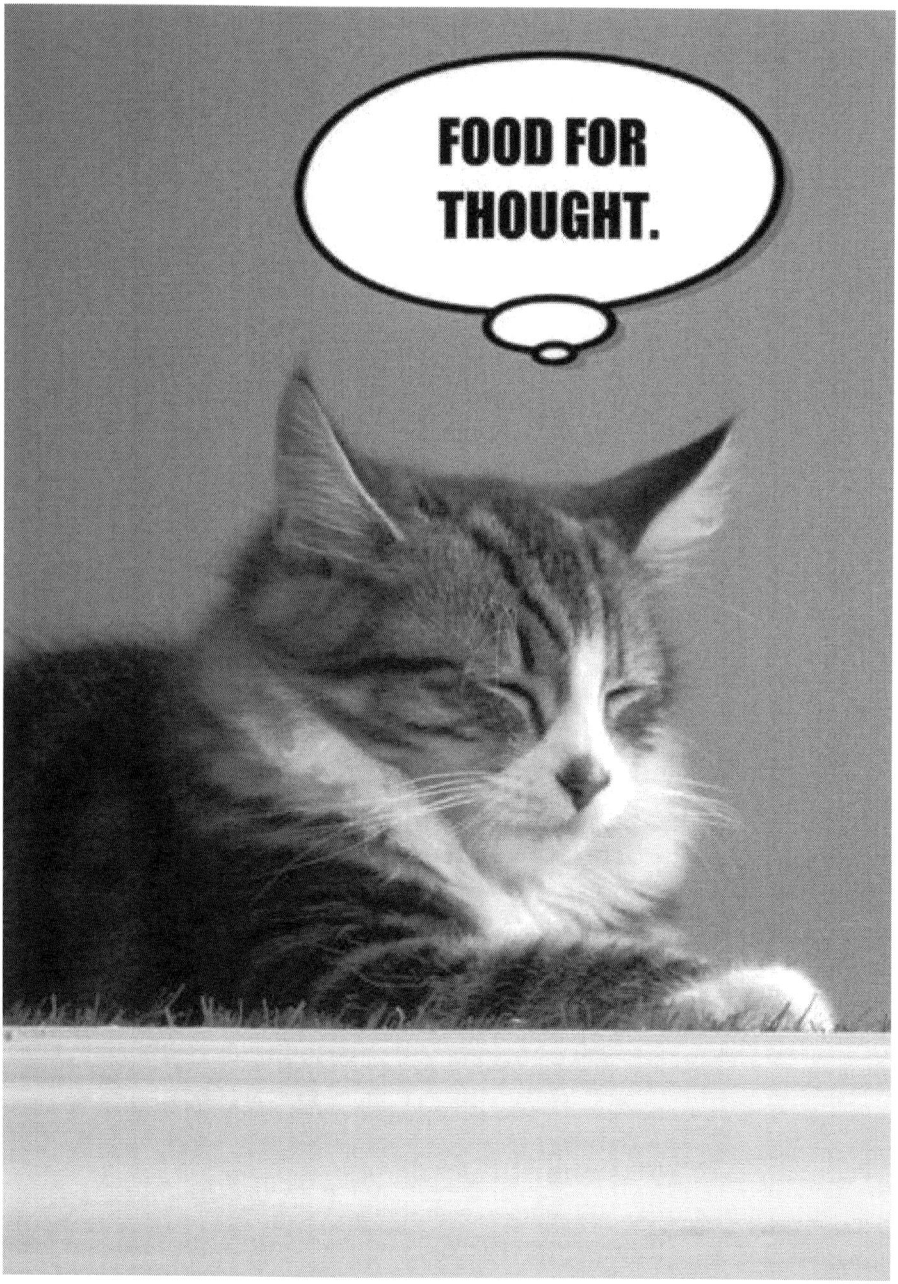
FOOD FOR THOUGHT.

Never cut or trim a cat's whiskers.
This can cause considerable upset
to the cat in question
and can even make her become
confused and disorientated.

A bowl is not the best kind of dish for a cat
to eat out of because her
whiskers will touch the sides
and annoy her while she is trying to eat.
A flat plate is much more comfortable for puss.

A cat's hearing is the best in the
whole of the animal kingdom.

A cat's mood is evident from the size of her pupils.
Full pupils mean a cat is excited or frightened,
narrow pupils mean she is angry.
However, her pupils
also react according to the amount of light available.

Cats only have 473 taste buds
compared to a human's 9,000 or so.

Cats must have fat in their food because
they cannot produce it themselves.

90 per cent of cats don't ever cross
busy roads.

A kitten's weight should double
in the first 14 days of her life.

Young kittens need to put on around 8-10g
weight every day.

Female cats can travel through territory
owned by multiple males without any trouble.

Most cats in the UK are allowed outside,
whereas most cats in the US are kept
as indoor only creatures.

When their ginger tom called Sandy went missing
from his family's home in Lee-On-Solent,
they put up missing posters and did all the usual
things to try to find him.
They were quite surprised
when he eventually turned up...in Spain.

Cats need 10 times more protein
than dogs.

You should never give your cat onions,
garlic, grapes, mushrooms,
chocolate or raisins.

If you put a towel at the bottom
of the bucket or bath
you're using to bath your cat, she will feel
more secure and be less likely to slip.

In Caledonia in the US, there is a
cat sanctuary where rescued domestic
moggies live alongside rescued big cats.

Clicker training was invented in the 1950s
and was originally created for
marine animals.

Cartoon kitty Garfield has appeared in some
128 newspapers across the world.

There is a town in America called Catskills.
Each Spring a new litter of some 240 cat statues
are placed up and down Main Street and are
a huge tourist attraction. At the end of the season,
they are auctioned off for charity.

Cat owners who show their cats can spend
£40,000 ($70,000) and upwards a year on travel
and grooming their pampered pusses.

MOST POPULAR CAT NAMES 2011

Female

1. Bella
2. Lucy
3. Kitty
4. Chloe
5. Sophie
6. Lily
7. Luna
8. Lilly
9. Callie
10. Daisy

Male

1. Max
2. Oliver
3. Charlie
4. Tiger
5. Smokey
6. Jack
7. Milo
8. Simba

9. Tigger
10. Kitty

2011 saw the debut of the female name Luna (from Harry Potter) and many other cat names were influenced by popular movies. Bella was the top female name for both cats and dogs, inspired by the Twilight series. It's been the top name for female cats since 2007 and female dogs since 2006. Lily and Lilly are believed to be inspired by characters on Modern Family and Gossip Girl.

Source: Vetstreet

More than a third of cats are believed
to be obese.

A cat is classified as obese if she
is 20 per cent or more over her
ideal weight.

The average cat needs to eat 200
calories a day.

Fat in cats tends to settle in the area
above the hips.

Thirty per cent of a cat's diet should
be made up of protein.

Experts recommend that you should
spend at least thirty minutes every day
playing with your cat/s.

If you have a cat that is aggressive or exhibits
destructive behaviour,
try playing with her every day
until she is completely exhausted. This will
usually fix the problems.

Great toys for wearing your kitty out include
Da Bird, red laser pointers, ping pong
balls and 'race tracks' with a ball trapped inside.

If they are introduced to each other at a young
enough age, cats can befriend smaller animals
that would normally be 'prey' like rats and mice.

In the US, there are 12 colleges that allow
students to live with their cats on campus.

You should avoid using ammonia
based products when
cleaning up cat pee. Ammonia smells
very similar to cats and will not stop them
returning to that spot
for another go.

The most common reason that cats spray urine
around the house is that they feel threatened
by the presence of one or more other cats
around or in their territory.

A male cat's roaming range is four
times larger than a female's.

One of the reasons cats groom themselves
is because it stimulates blood flow around the body.

Cats will groom each other as a sign of friendship.

One male calico cat is born for every 3,000 females.

Cats enjoy lying in the sun so much
because they are originally desert animals.

Cats learn to purr very early on in their lives.
They start purring at about one week old.

The younger a cat is, the faster her little heart beats.

Cats scratch to show other cats
very visually that this is their territory.

Cats will prefer to scratch in 'high traffic'
areas (places where people often go),
so place scratching posts in these areas for best results.

If you have problems with your
cat waking you up first thing
in the morning for breakfast,
try feeding her last thing at night instead.

A cat's collarbone is not connected to any of her
other bones, which enables
her to squeeze through
any opening as long as her head can get through.

Unlike dogs, when a cat wags her tail
she's not pleased to see you. She's upset.

Cats have 38 chromosomes,
just like their closest wild ancestors.

The average litter is two to six kittens.

According to ancient Chinese legends,
cats can see ghosts.

A female cat can have three to five litters a year.

Indoor cats live longer than outdoor cats.

There are more than 35,000 kittens
born in the US every year.

Domestic cats love surveying the world
from high places,
much like their wild ancestors
leopards and jaguars.

Cats don't like loud noises. This is probably
because their hearing
is so much more sensitive than ours.

Less than one per cent of the
total cat population is purebred.

Anyone who's watched a
cat take a tumble indoors
will know that it's not true
that a cat will always land on her feet.

The calico cat is the official cat of the state of Maryland.

The first animated cat cartoon was Krazy Kat.

MOST POPULAR CAT NAMES 2012

Female

1. Bella
2. Kitty
3. Lucy
4. Chloe
5. Luna
6. Sophie
7. Lily
8. Daisy
9. Lilly
10. Callie

Male

1. Max
2. Oliver
3. Tiger
4. Simba
5. Charlie
6. Milo
7. Smokey
8. Jack

9. Leo
10. Kitty

Other popular names that didn't quite make the top 10 included Katniss (after the star of The Hunger Games), Loki and Thor (from The Avengers) and Stella, Willow, Rosie, Minnie, Oscar, Louie and Blue.

Source: Vetstreet

Michael Stipe of the rock band REM
has a tattoo of Krazy Kat and
the object of his unrequited affection, Igntaz Mouse.

Many artists have immortalized cats
on canvas in their works.
These include Manet, Renoir, Goya and Warhol.

The longest ever whisker measured
was 7.5 inches long
and was attached to a cat from Finland.

The base pigments of black and orange
form the basis for all the different coat colours
of the domestic cat.

A male cat that has been neutered is called a gib.

Chocolate can be toxic to both cats and dogs.
Save it for yourself.

An Indonesian legend
says that cats can control the rain.

In 1994, archaeologists discovered the
remains of a cat buried

with a person that dated back to
the New Stone Age.
On the basis of this discovery,
it seems that some may
have been domesticated much earlier
than the Ancient Egyptian era.

The claw that is on the side of the cat's
front paws is called a dewclaw.

A cat's dewclaws are their
equivalents of our thumbs.
They use them for climbing trees
and grasping prey.

Cats make a distinctive chattering
noise when they
see something they want but know
that they can't have it - for example
a bird on the other side of a window.

THE INTERNET CAT VIDEO FESTIVAL – AN ACTUAL THING

There is an annual Internet Cat Video Festival that takes place every year. The idea came from 'unofficial cat lady in residence' at an art centre, Katie Hill, who originally suggested it as a joke.

The first Internet Cat Video Festival was held at the Walker Art Centre in Minneapolis in 2012 and attracted 10,000 people to the venue to watch and vote on their favourite viral cat videos.

Katie Hill, who by now was probably regretting the whole idea, watched through over 10,000 submitted cat videos to select a 65 minute showreel for the event.

The public were invited to vote on their
favourite video to be given
the 'Golden Kitty' award.
Will Braden won with his two minute video
titled 'Henri 2, Paw de Deux.' It was the second
video featuring melancholy cat
Henri Le Chat Noir
lamenting his meaningless existence.

After the main event on August 30, 2012,
the Internet Cat Video Festival went on tour,
stopping off to bring silly cat videos to
places like Boston, Memphis and Vienna.

The 2013 festival also featured a cat
sculpture made entirely out of butter.
It took artists two days to make.
Why did they do it?
I honestly have no idea.

The festivals are often graced with real-life guest
appearances from celebrity cats and their owners,
like Grumpy Cat, Lil BUB and Dusty the Klepto Kitty.

Many of the Internet Cat Video Festivals aim
to help raise money for cat charities
and have adoption booths, as well as
live music, fancy dress competitions,
art projects and other madness.

It is believed that there are a total of
some 500 million domestic cats worldwide.

The musical Cats spent 18 years on Broadway.
It was the longest-running show until
Phantom of the Opera knocked it off the top spot.

Over 3,000 pounds of Yak hair has been used
over the years to make the wigs for the Cats musical.

An estimated 200,000 to 300,000 feral cats
live in Rome and roam the Eternal City.

A law passed in Rome in the 1990s
give stray cats the right to remain
in the place where they were born.

Number 10 Downing Street has a tradition
dating back 200 years of having
a cat about the house.

FAMOUS CAT LOVERS...

UK Prime Minister Winston Churchill was particularly fond of cats. Here's a picture of him petting Blackie, the mascot of HMS Prince of Wales.

It was taken in August 1941. During a meeting with President Roosevelt, Churchill bent down to give Blackie a friendly pat on the head. He was later lambasted by the Cats Protective League, which scolded him by stating, "He should have conformed to the

etiquette demanded by the occasion,
offering his hand
and then awaiting a sign of approval
before taking liberties."
Blackie declined to comment.

Churchill also owned dogs, including a poodle called Rufus.

Churchill was given a ginger and white cat for his
88th birthday. He named him Jock and his new
kitty would travel with the elderly gentleman
when he travelled from his home
in Chartwell to London.

When Churchill died, the National Trust took
over Chartwell, and his family asked that there
always be a marmalade cat called Jock on the premises.

Churchill's most famous cat was one he kept
during the war called Nelson. He was a big grey fellow
and Churchill once described him as
the bravest cat he ever knew.
Once he chased a much bigger dog away.

Physicist Albert Einstein loved animals,
and owned a tomcat called Tiger,
who was depressed by rain.

Author of Les Miserables Victor Hugo wrote
often in his diary about his love of cats.

Beatle John Lennon loved cats
since he was a little boy.
He called his first cat Mimi and
kept a horde of cats
when he lived with his first wife Cynthia.
He also enjoyed drawing pictures of kitties,
some of which are published in his books.

Nurse Florence Nightingale owned some 60 cats
during her life, including a huge Persian she named Bismarck.

Domestic goddess Martha Stewart
shares her home
with a number of cats.
She owns two calico Persians
named Empress Tang and Princess Peony
and six blue-point
Himalayans called Frost, Snow, Bartok,
Verdi, Vivaldi and Mozart.

Inventor Nikola Tesla became
fascinated with electricity
after seeing sparks fly when he
stroked his cat Macak.

Author H G Wells owned a cat he called
Mr Peter Wells. Peter didn't like people
talking too loudly, and when someone
would do so,
he would protest angrily about it before
leaving the room.

French cake-eating
Queen Marie Antoinette adored
her Angora cats and gave
them free run of her palace.
They would meander around
the tables during court gatherings.

The three Bronte sisters, Charlotte, Emily and
Anne were all cat lovers.

Crime writer Raymond Chandler owned a black
Persian called Taki and nicknamed her his 'secretary'
due to her habit of sitting on his manuscripts
while he was trying to edit them.

Many famous artists were known to be cat lovers,
including Henri Matisse,
Gustav Klimt, Pierre Auguste
Renoir and Claude Monet.

You probably wouldn't have guessed it from
his name, but rap star Snoop Dogg is a cat man.
He owns a whole gang of kitties, including two
Siamese called Frank Sinatra and Miles Davis.

Cats and writers have a long history together.
Some well-known writers who fancied felines
include Paul Gallico, Walter de la Mare,
Thomas Hardy, Edward Lear, Lewis Carroll,
Beatrix Potter and W B Yeats.

The actress Halle Berry played Catwoman in the
2004 film, and during filming fell in love with
one of the 43 cats that were
her co-workers on the film.
She called her new puss Play Dough.

Songstress Katy Perry has a cat
she calls Kitty Purry.
She misses him terribly
when she is away on tour.

Katy's ex-husband Russell Brand
is also a cat man.
He owns a cat called Morrissey after the
Smiths frontman.
When Katy Perry and Kitty Purry
moved in, Morrissey was about as happy as his
namesake. Russell had to call a pet
therapist, who prescribed valium.

Morrissey himself is also a cat fan and has owned
several different felines over the years.

Writer William S Boroughs' wrote in his final
journal entry about how much he loved his cats.
He wrote, "Pure love – what I feel
for my cats present and past. Love?
What is it? Most
natural painkiller there is."

Charles Dickens was also a cat lover.
When his cat Bob
died in 1862, he had the cat's paw stuffed and
mounted on the end of a letter opener.
You can see it, if you really want to,
on display in the Berg Collection of English
and American Literature at the
New York Public Library.

Sandman author Neil Gaiman is another cat man.
He owns several felines with names
like Hermione, Pod,
Zoe and Princess. His beloved cat
Zoe died earlier
this year (2014) and
Neil is said to be heartbroken.

French novelist Colette has been
called 'the original
catwoman' because of her intense
adoration for cats.
She also wrote a book titled 'The Cat'.

Joyce Carol Oates has written over fifty novels,
and perhaps she is so prolific because she simply
HATES to get up when her kitty sits on
her lap and purrs.

Comedian Ricky Gervais
often posts selfies of himself
and his blue-eyed Siamese cat Ollie on Twitter.

Singer Patti Smith is another cat fan. In the 2008 documentary about her titled 'Patti Smith: Dream of Life' one of her kitties makes an appearance.

Actor James Dean also liked cats and kept a pet Siamese called Marcus, who was a present from actress Elizabeth Taylor.

Previous Pope Pope Benedict XVI made no secret of the fact that he loved cats, and when he was no longer pope, one of the benefits was that he was able to finally own one. Popes are not allowed to have them in residence in the Vatican.

Japanese author Haruki Murakami manages to get cats into all of his books somewhere, often as guides for other characters. He also named his Tokyo jazz bar Peter Cat after a real cat called Peter.

Author Terry Pratchett is fond of cats, as readers have probably been able to guess from his books, including one called 'The Unadulterated Cat'. He passed on his affection of felines to his daughter, video game writer Rhianna Pratchett, who owns two pure white coloured kitties.

Singer Lisa Loeb admits that she can't help petting cats that she sees on the street, even though she knows that she probably shouldn't.

Pop star Dusty Springfield loved all animals, but was particularly delighted by cats.

During her life, she
was an advocate for many
animal protection groups.

Actress Tricia Helfer has a
menagerie of 10 rescue
cats to keep her
company at home in Los Angeles.

Another actress who loves the company of cats is
Chloe Sevigny. She thinks cats are 'really freaky
and weird and powerful and wild.'

Les Mis author Victor Hugo had a cat
called Gavroche
which he later renamed Chanoine
('because of his
indolence and idleness') and
another called Mouche.

Egyptian Queen Cleopatra reportedly had 14 cats,
and her favourite was a mog called Tivali.

During her childhood, Queen Victoria was
isolated from other people and instead made
friendships with dolls and pets. She
owned two blue Persian cats and was enchanted
by them. Seeing their Queen's love of cats,
much of the country
also fell in love with them.

Whatever you think of her politics, you can't fault
ex PM Margaret Thatcher on her love of cats.
She adopted a tabby cat from the
Mayhew Animal Home
to keep her company after
the death of her husband.
She reportedly would have
liked to have owned pets

earlier in her life, but her son Mark
and her husband weren't amenable to the idea.

Other famous cat lovers include
chemist Louis Pasteur,
actress Doris Day, author C. S. Lewis,
King Henry VIII, comedian Bill Cosby,
actor Robert Redford and writers Kingsley Amis,
P. J. O'Rourke, A. A. Milne and Doris Lessing

...AND FAMOUS CAT HATERS

Alexander the Great liked
breeding fearsome war dogs
but had no time for cats. He was well known
for setting his dogs upon any cat he saw while
he was out walking them.

Nazi party leader Adolf Hitler was more of a
dog person. He owned a German Shepherd
he called Blondi who sometimes even
slept on his master's bed
with him. However, his loyalty was
hardly rewarded – when Hitler wanted to check
that his cyanide pills worked, he tested
one on Blondi to find out.

Hitler's mistress, Eva Braun,
was herself a cat lover,
although she knew better than to argue
with the Fruher about which pet to keep
at home. She would occasionally
kick the dog under the table when Hitler
wasn't looking.

Queen Elizabeth I was believed to not
be incredibly fond of felines.

Composer Johannes Brahms
sounds like he was a
charming man. One of his favourite
hobbies was to sit
at an open window and try to
kill local cats with a
bow and arrow.

Former US President Dwight D. Eisenhower also
had an intense dislike of cats. He gave his staff

strict orders to shoot any that were unfortunate enough to wander onto the White House grounds.

Ruthless Italian dictator Benito Mussolini also hated cats. In 1936, journalist John Gunter wrote of him, 'The things that Mussolini hates most are Hitler, aristocrats, money, cats and old age.'

Genghis Khan had a terrible fear of cats. So does LaToya Jackson.

Henry III was so terrified of cats that he was known to faint if one so much as came near him.

Another 'fearless' leader who was actually frightened of cats was Napoleon Bonaparte. He was once found sweating profusely and lunging wildly with his sword. What was he so afraid of? A little tiny kitten.

Roman general Julius Caesar was also unfortunate enough to suffer from a fear of cute little kittens.

Roman Emperor Nero is believed to be another bad guy who –coincidentally, we're sure – happens to hate cats.

A surprising name on this list is that of poet Emily Dickinson. She disliked the way that her sister's cat would hunt and kill other wildlife while she was looking out into her garden.

Another surprise would be author J R R Tolkien, who was said to not be so fond of felines.

Although our last Pope loved cats, others weren't so keen. Cat haters include Pope Gregory IX, Pope Innocent VIII and Pope Innocent VII.

A modern day famous cat hater is rumoured to be Tea Party politician Sarah Palin.

English naturalist Chris Packham is not keen on cats at all. He believes that they are decimating the local bird population and should be kept as indoor only pets or have a night time curfew.

All things considered, I think the cat lovers are a better lot than the cat haters, don't you?

The world's oldest known statue is of a cat.
The Lion Man is believed to be 32,000 years old
and was found in a cave in Southern Germany.

The Egyptian Queen Cleopatra
had a pet kitty called Charmian.
She thought her cat
was so pretty that she tried to make her eyes
mimic hers with her trademark eyeliner.

Li Shou was a feline fertility goddess
worshipped by the ancient Chinese.

A 29-year old man in Lancashire
called Louis Denyer
claims that he has taught himself to speak
fluently with cats.

A new cat feeder called the Bistro is coming after
a successful crowdfunding
campaign on Indiegogo.
The Bistrot identifies cats using facial recognition
to make sure the right puss is eating its food.
It will also check up on kitty's health,
weight and hydration.

Grumpy Cat's real name is Tardar Sauce
and she's female.

In New York, cats have their own cafe
called The Meow Mix Cafe. It's not a traditional
cat café as such, but a place where people
can bring their own cats and have a coffee.

There is a book called How To Make Your
Cat An Internet Celebrity. It's authored by
Patricia Carlin and Dustin Fenstermacher
and you can buy it on Amazon.

If you're a guy, you'll be pleased to know
that there is a book called
Guys Can Be Cat Ladies Too.
It's by Michael Showalter and you can also
buy it online.

One of the most amusingly titled cat books ever,
Games You Can Play With Your Pussy – by
Ira Alterman and Marty Riskin is also available.

You can also buy a cat themed Bible. Titled
The LOLcat Bible by Martin Grondin, it contains
such lines as 'At start, no has lite.
An Ceiling Cat says,
I can haz lite? An lite wuz.'

Lions and tigers can mate and successfully
give birth to offspring.
The love child of a male lion
and female tiger is called a liger.

Ligers are extremely rare and
there are only twelve
or so of them in existence in the whole world,
and all of those are in captivity.

If a male tiger mates with a female lion,
the resulting offspring is called a tigon.

The word **PURR** in different languages:

Afrikaans: gonzen
Albanian: kerrmez
Azerbaijani: tirilti
Basque: purra
Belarusian: murlykac
Bulgarian: murkane
Catalan: ronc
Chinese: fachu hou yin
Croatian: presti
Czech: prist
Danish: spindle
Dutch: spinnen
Estonian: nurrumine
Filipino: bahagyang huni
Finnish: kehrata
French: ronronner
Galician: ronronar
German: schnurren
Hawaiian: nonolo
Haitian Creole: ronron
Hebrew: yeemyom
Hindi: myaum

Hungarian: dorombol
Icelandic: mala
Indonesian: dengung
Italian: fusa
Japanese: gorogoro
Korean: degul degul
Latvian: nurrat
Lithuanian: murkti
Macedonian: preda
Malay: dengung
Polish: mruczec
Portuguese: ronronar
Romanian: tors
Russian: orchetz
Serbian: mrrrr
Slovakian: pradenia
Slovenian: presti
Spanish: ronroneo
Swedish: spinna
Thai: seiyng fi xyang maew
Turkish: mirlamak
Vietnamese: zen ghu ghu
Welsh: Grwnan
Yiddish: prr

Tigons tend to be smaller than
either of their parents,
whereas ligers can grow to massive sizes.
The average liger stands 12 feet tall
and weighs 1,000 pounds.

Tigons are even rarer than ligers
as male tigers only very, very seldom
feel the love for female lions.

More than 20 species of
wild cats (including snow leopards and
mountain lions) are now on the
US Fish and Wildlife Service's
threatened and endangered list.

Approximately one cat in 20 has feline asthma.

Cats have a total of 517 muscles in their tiny bodies.

An adult lion's roar is so loud
that it can be heard up to five miles away.

A tiger's stripes are completely
unique to each tiger.

No two are ever the same and they can be
likened to human fingerprints
for identification purposes.

Fossils have been found of jaguars
that are some two million years old.

Unlike all other cats, lions have a distinctive
tuft of hair at the end of their tails.

Lions will only manage to make a successful kill
one out of every five attempts,
so a big part of their
diet revolves around scavenging.

Lions can be identified by their whisker spots.
These are unique to each lion.

For every 3,000 times a male lion has sex,
one cub will successfully be born and survive
to reach one year old. Those are
terrible odds!

Tigers have the longest life span of all the big cats,
and can live to up to 26 years in the wild.

Female tigers reach puberty somewhere
between three and four years old,
whereas male tigers
mature at between four and five years.

Snow leopards have uniquely large nasal cavities,
which help them to breathe the thin air up in the mountains.

White tigers appear due to a recessive gene
which is carried by the Bengal tiger.

A jaguar is capable of biting down with its teeth
with a force of 2000 pounds. This gives it the
strongest gnashers of any cat.

A lion's pride is made up of around 30 different lions.

The size of a lion's pride is determined by
how much food and water is available.
The less is around, the smaller the pride will be.

A male lion's thick mane protects his
vulnerable neck when he is fighting.

Male lions don't do very much. Female lions
do most of the hunting and do so
in packs to bring down prey.

The lion's digestive system allows them to eat
and eat and eat when food is available,
allowing them to survive for longer
on nothing when it is not.

A cat is called a feral cat
when it is the same species
as a domestic cat but has not had experience
of humans in its crucial socialization
period as a kitten.

A stray cat, on the other hand, is a cat
who used to be a pet but has strayed
from or left its home for some reason. These
kitties can happily become pets again
with the right people.

There is a colony of 10,000 feral cats in Florida.

Very few feral kittens survive.

Feral cats tend to live close to sources of food, for example near restaurants, blocks of flats and hotels.

MOST POPULAR CAT NAMES 2013

Female

1. Bella
2. Lucy
3. Kitty
4. Luna
5. Chloe
6. Molly
7. Lily
8. Sophie
9. Nala
10. Daisy

Male

1. Oliver
2. Max
3. Tiger
4. Charlie
5. Simba
6. Milo
7. Smokey
8. Leo

9. Jack
10. Kitty

Max was knocked off the top spot for male cats after a five year run and Oliver snuck in to replace it. Other names that have gained massively in popularity in 2013, despite not making the top 10 are Mittens, which jumped from 28 to 18 and Pepper, which pounced from 42 to 21.

Source: Vetstreet

The most common food for feral cats is food taken from rubbish bins.

There are four different types of tabby cats - mackerel, classic, spotted and ticked.

There are three major different shapes of cat heads - there's the triangle shape that Siamese have, the round heads like Persians and the rectangular like Maine Coons have.

Most moggies will have a triangular shaped head.

Female cats tend to be better hunters.

The sharp angles of the cat's hind legs help give power to her sprinting, climbing and jumping.

Japanese sailors have more cats on board their ships than any other nationality.

Hindus believe that they must stroke at least one cat during their lifetime.

In continental Europe, it is believed that if a
house cat was a gift, it will bring good luck to
the members of the household,
but if she was bought,
she will just be an ordinary pet.

A reason people often give for
not committing suicide
when they are feeling low is
that they are worried
about what will happen to their cat or
other pet once they are gone.

Feline stars, just like their human actor
and actress counterparts, also have agents.

Even cats that have been declawed
(a process that is
illegal in the UK but still practiced
widely in the US)
will go through the motions of scratching.

An old superstition is that when a cat sneezes,
it is soon going to rain.

When pumas are born they have spots
on their coat and deep blue eyes.

Leopards are sometimes nicknamed
the 'prima ballerina' and the 'prince of cats'.

Snow leopards have exceptionally large paws,
which allow them to walk on top of snow
as if they were wearing snowshoes.

Although the lion is often
called the 'King of the Jungle'
they don't actually live in the jungle.

Their natural habitat is the grassy plains
of east and south Africa.

Leopards are so strong they can climb up a tree
carrying prey twice their weight in their jaws.

In one single stride, a cheetah can
cover some 23 to 26 feet.

Cheetah is the Hindi word for 'spotted one'.

All cheetahs have the same blood type
and can donate organs and blood to any other cheetah.

Big cat circus trainers can teach their lions
and tigers to use (big) litter boxes.

The leopard is the most widespread of all the big cats.

The serval is the best cat at hunting.
They are successful
at catching their prey between
40 to 60 per cent of the time.

Wild cats do not bury their poop -
unless they are
very timid. In fact, most of them
deliberately leave
it out in the open to mark their territory.

Big cats can gain as much as a pound a day
in weight between the ages of one and two.

Big cats have an acute sense of hearing
and a mother cat can hear one of her cubs crying
from anything up to a mile away.

On every lap of water, a domestic cat manages
to imbibe 0.1 millimetres of liquid. She averages
four laps per second, so that's only 5 teaspoons a minute.

According to the American Association for Pet
Obesity Prevention, pets are getting fatter
along with people. Around 54 per cent
of America's pets are obese,
which makes for approximately 50 million fat cats.

Cats have better muscle memory than visual memory.

There are five different species of
tiger - Siberian, Indochinese, South Chinese,
Bengal and Sumatran.

After enjoying a meal, a lion can drink
solidly for a whole thirty minutes.

The distinctive black lines on a cheetah's face
are called tears. It's believed that they help to
block out the bright glare of the sun.

Not all Manx cats have no tail at all.
Some of them have a short stub while others have
normal length, magnificent tails.

The five rarest wildcats are, the Bornean Bay cat,
the Flat-headed cat, the Snow Leopard,
the Andean mountain cat and the Iberian Lynx.

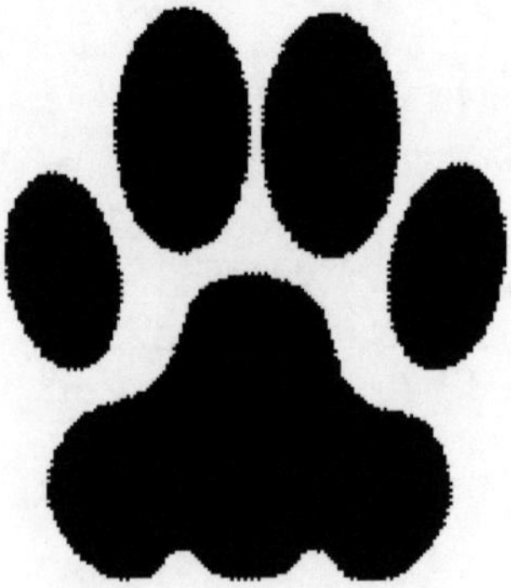

CAT DREAMS EXPLAINED! *

(* possibly)

Just for fun, here are some interpretations of what it means when you dream about cats or kittens. Take them all with a pinch of salt.

If you dream about newborn kittens, or kittens that are loudly mewing it can mean that you feel vulnerable and need help that doesn't seem to be forthcoming.

Kittens can also represent a new project that you've started that needs a lot of effort and work to get off the ground.

Some people believe that when a woman dreams about cats, the cats represent how she sees herself.

A healthy, pampered cat means that the woman has a lot of self confidence and a mangy stray the exact opposite.

When men dream about cats, it's thought that they represent his attitude towards women.

If, in a man's dream, the cat is purring and rubbing herself against the dreamer, the man is used to getting a lot of positive attention from women and also likely feels comfortable in female company.

However, if the cat is hissing, scratching and/or running away from him, this is supposed to mean that the dreamer feels rejected by women and doesn't really understand them or get on with them very well.

A cat can also represent the dreamer's intuition. Did you ignore the cat or pay attention to it? That could mean that you follow or ignore your own intuition accordingly.

A dream about a sick cat or cats can mean you're not properly listening to that little voice inside your head, especially if you do nothing about the poor state of the feline.

A cat can also represent a person in your life who is 'catty' and malicious. Have a think - do you have anyone in your life that that could be?

If the cat in your dream has no tail, it means that you feel as if you have lost your independence and autonomy.

A white cat means that difficult times are on their way.

A black cat can mean that you are afraid of your own psychic ability.

Dreaming of a cat killing a spider is supposed to mean that you are expressing your feminine side in a seductive and cunning manner.

If you see cats playing, it means you should relax and let yourself have more fun.

If you dream of yourself as having cat's eyes, it means that you are currently in the midst of solving a dark and troubling problem.

If the cat is scared, then you might be being a bit mean to your friends and should try harder to be nice to them.

Being on the receiving end of a cat bite can mean you feel like you've been less than tactful recently.

Big cats can get hairballs
just like domestic cats do.
Try to avoid them when
they're coughing them up.

A hapless lion from one of the UK's safari parks
had to have emergency surgery to remove a
particularly troublesome hairball in 2009.

The Asian Mountaineer cat has the thickest
and longest fur of all the wild cats,
probably because
it needs to get through the
bitterly cold winters in its natural habitat.

There are more tigers now living in
captivity than in the wild.

Cats have different coloured patches of skin
not just patches of fur.

A tiger's paw prints are called pug marks.

The Harrods shop in Knightsbridge
used to have a zoo

in its flagship store. Among other animals,
they once had two lion cubs for sale.

According to publishers, books about cats,
or with pictures of cats on the cover sell better
than other books. I've done both to cover my bases.

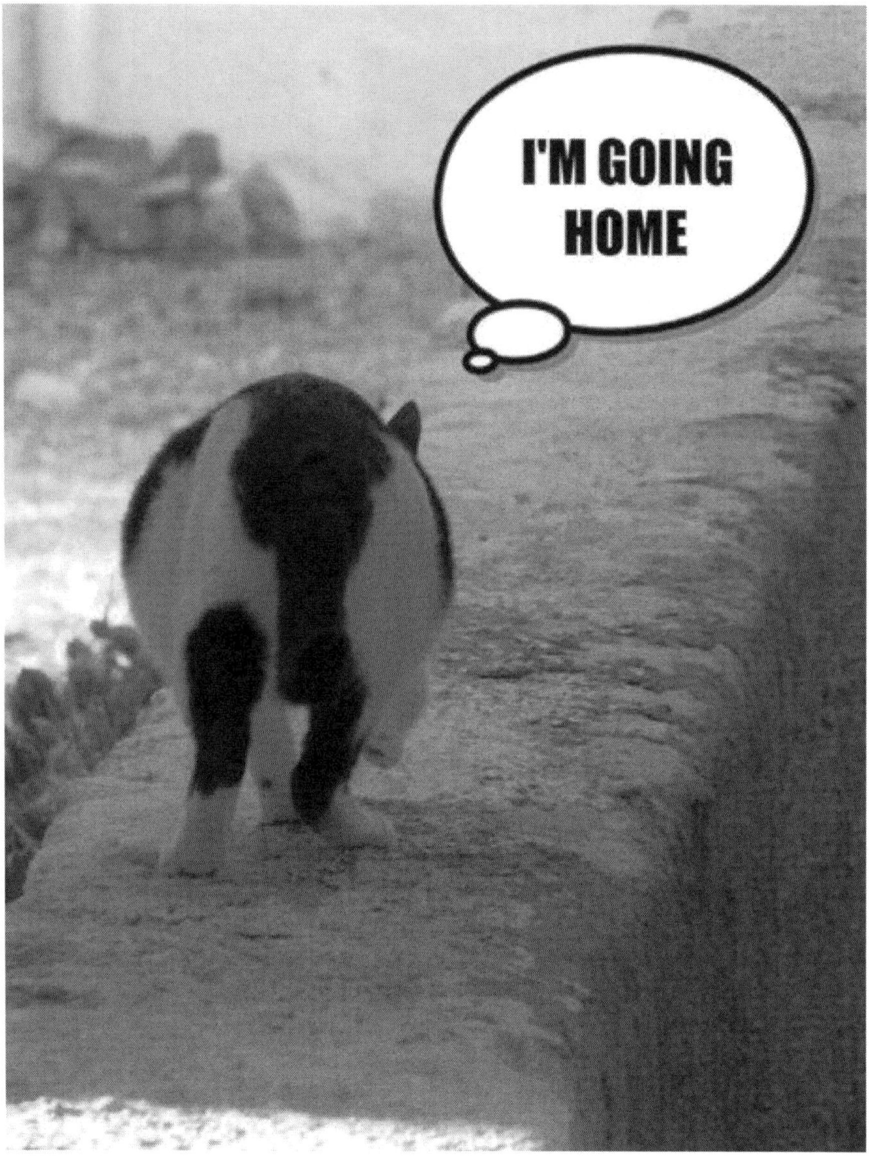
I'M GOING HOME

FINAL NOTE

If you love cats and have a bit of cash to spare, why not make a donation to one of the following cat charities? I know people who work for them all personally and have seen them hard at work first hand. None of them have CEOs with six-figure salaries, 'boards of directors' with bloated salaries or any such rubbish. Any money you give will genuinely go to helping down on their luck kitties.

YORKSHIRE CAT RESCUE
A lovely little rescue centre for cats and kittens in Yorkshire and parts of Lancashire – although if you don't mind travelling up (or down) there to meet their residents, you can adopt from anywhere in the UK.
yorkshirecatrescue.org

ROMNEY HOUSE CAT RESCUE
Another great rescue centre, this one based in Downe in Kent and homing cats to London and the South East, Romney House also cares for a number of 'unadoptable' cats on its sprawling premises, permanent residents with problems which mean they are unlikely to ever find a happy home. You can make a general donation or choose one of these critters to sponsor for a year.
www.romneyhousecatrescue.org.uk

NINE LIVES GREECE
A group of volunteers who look after the many, many homeless cats that roam the streets of Greece. They fund and perform trap, neuter and release programs and provide food and veterinary care for as many pussycats as they can. They also have some special cats that are up for adoption to overseas homes, providing you're promising them a happy forever home.
www.ninelivesgreece.com

SANTORINI ANIMAL WELFARE ASSOCIATION
The beautiful Greek Island of Santorini is home to many stray animals and this rescue organization helps care for them,

particularly during the off season when many of the restaurants and bars close down. SAWA looks after not only stray cats, but stray dogs and donkeys, too.
www.sawasantorini.org

LUFTI'S LEGACY
Not an official charity, just an arty cat owner called Inez Thomson who lost her beloved feline Lufti to Feline Infectious Peritonitis (FIP). This devastating disease can not be vaccinated against and Inez decided to try to raise money to put towards more research into this field by selling her own handmade catnip toys (I can vouch for the Halloween themed pumpkins – my two went nuts over them).
https://www.facebook.com/groups/1432630666969659/

BIBLIOGRAPHY

Allred, Alexandra Powe. *Cats' Most Wanted The Top 10 Book Of Mysterious Mousers, Talented Tabbies, And Feline Oddities*. Washington, D.C.: Potomac Books, 2005. Print.

Anderson, Janice. *The Cat-A-Logue*. Enfield: Guinness Books, 1987. Print.

Becker, Marty, and Gina Spadafori. *Do Cats Always Land On Their Feet?: 101 Of The Most Perplexing Questions Answered About Feline Unfathomables, Medical Mysteries & Befuddling Behaviors*. Deerfield Beach, Fla.: Health Communications, 2006. Print.

Becker, Marty, and Gina Spadafori. *MeowWow: Curiously Compelling Facts, True Tales, And Trivia Even Your Cat Won't Know*. Deerfield Beach, FL: Health Communications, 2007. Print.

Carter, Seanbaker. *Must Love Cats*. Animal Planet. 2011. Television.

Choron, Sandra, Harry Choron, and Arden Moore. *Planet Cat: A Cat-Alog*. Boston: Houghton Mifflin Co., 2007. Print.

Church, Christine. *House Cat: How To Keep You Indoor Cat Sane And Sound*. Howell Book House, 2005. Print.

Cook, Gladys Emerson, and Felix Sutton. *The Big Book Of Cats*. New York: Grossett & Dunlap, 1954. Print.

Davidson, Catherine. *Why does my CAT do that?* Ivy Press, 2014. Print.

Diego, Calif. *Uncle John's Bathroom Reader Cat Lover's Companion*. San Diego, CA: Portable Press, 2006. Print.

Evans, Rod L., and Irwin M. Berent. *The ABC Of Cat Trivia.* New York: St. Martin's Press, 1996. Print.

Factly, IP. *101 Facts...CATS!* Amazon Kindle, 2014. Ebook.

Hampshire, Kristen, Iris Bass, and Lori Paximadis. *Cat Lover's Daily Companion: 365 Days Of Insight And Guidance For Living A Joyful Life With Your Cat.* Beverly, Mass.: Quarry Books, 2009. Print.

Keens-Soper, Alice. *The Secret Life Of...Cats.* Oxford Scientific Films, 2014. Television.

Lang, Stephen J. *1,001 Things You Always Wanted To Know About Cats.* Howell Book House, 2004. Print.

Leese, Ian. *Joanna Lumley: Catwoman.* ITV Studios, 2009. Television.

Laroche, Robert de., and Jean Labat. *The Secret Life Of Cats.* Hauppauge, NY: Barron's, 1995. Print.

Mara, Lesley. *Cats Miscellany: Everything You Always Wanted To Know About Our Feline Friends.* New York: Skyhorse Pub., 2011. Print.

Martyn, Elizabeth. *Everything Cats Expect You To Know.* Intercourse, PA: Good Books, 2008. Print.

Moore, Arden, and Arden Moore. *Happy Cat, Happy You: Quick Tips For Building A Bond With Your Feline Friend.* North Adams, MA: Storey Pub., 2008. Print.

Moore, Joan. *The Cat Lover's Companion.* Montreal: Tormont, 19931992. Print.

Neill, Amanda. *Cat Biz.* Hauppauge, N.Y.: Barron's, 20072006. Print.

Page, Jake. *Do Cats Hear With Their Feet?*. HarperCollins, 2009. Print.

Pirincİşci, Akif, and Rolf Degen. *Cat Sense: Inside The Feline Mind*. London: Fourth Estate, 1994. Print.

Richter, Jack. *Your Talking Cat*. Chelmsford: The Windsor Group, 2005. Print.

Sage, Helen. *The Secret Life Of The Cat*. Horizon, 2013. Television.

Sands, David. *Cats: 500 Questions Answered*. London: Hamlyn, 2005. Print.

Werner, Trevor. *Cat Body Language Phrasebook: 100 Ways To Read Their Signals*. San Diego, Calif.: Thunder Bay Press, 2007. Print.

PICTURE CREDITS

Cat silhouettes all from Wikimedia Commons. Walking Cat Silhouette by Persian Poet Gal. Sitting Cat Silhouette by Booyabazooka. Paw print by OCAL. Stretching cat silhouette by rferran.

Winston Churchill and Blackie pic taken by Horton (Capt), War Office official photographer, from the collections of the Imperial War Museums.

Picture of Tama by Takobou.

Photo of Internet Cat Video Festival by Rachel Joyce for the Walker Art Center.

Cover design and photography by Damon Torsten Nash.

All other photographs by Emma Boyes and Damon Torsten Nash.

All rights reserved.

ABOUT THE AUTHOR

Emma Boyes is a full-time writer and journalist. She has written articles about all kinds of things for all kinds of places including Chat, Starburst, the Daily Mail, Metropolis, Japanzine, Woman's Own and Metro. She has also written the stories for various video games and spent two years on staff at GameSpot. A lifelong cat lover, after spending a decade living overseas, she's finally able to have two mogs of her own – a grumpy tabby called Athena and a bouncy Maine Coon called Izzy. She can be contacted at emmaboyes@gmail.com

APPENDIX : CATS BEWARE!

A surprising amount of things are poisonous to cats, possibly one reason why they tend to be such finicky eaters. Popular flowers like Lilies, Chrysanthemums and Daffodils are toxic to them – something I didn't know and almost learned the very hard way when one of mine became sick. It's worth having a complete list somewhere to reference.

FLOWERS WHICH ARE POISONOUS TO CATS:

Acocanthera
Aconite
Alfalfa
Almond (pits)
Aloe Vera
Alocasia
Alsike Clover
Amaryllis
Amsinckia
Angels Trumpet
Angels Wings
Apple (seeds)
Apple Leaf Croton
Apricot (Pits)
Arrowgrass
Arrowhead Vine
Asparagus Fern
Autumn Crocus
Avocado (fruit and pit)
Azalea

Baby's Breath
Baneberry
Bayonet
Beargrass
Beech
Belladonna

Bird of Paradise
Bitter Cherry
Bitter Nightshade
Bittersweet
Black-eyed Susan
Black Locust
Bleeding Heart
Bloodroot
Bluebonnet
Blue Flag
Blue-Green Algae
Boston Ivy
Bouncing Bet
Box
Boxwood
Brackenfern
Brake Fern
Branching Ivy
Buckeyes
Buddhist Pine
Bull Nettle
Burning Bush
Buttercup

Cactus
Candelabra
Caladium
Caley Pea
Calfkill
Calla Lily
Candelabra Cactus
Castorbean
Ceriman
Chalice Vine
Charming Dieffenbachia
Chinaberry tree
Chinese Evergreen
Chinese Inkberry
Christmas Plant

Christmas Rose
Chrysanthemum
Cineria
Clematis
Climbing Nightshade
Clover
Cocklebur
Common Burdock
Common Privet
Common Tansy
Coral Plant
Cordalis
Cordatum
Coriaria
Cornflower
Corn Plant
Cornstalk Plant
Cowslip
Crabs Eye
Croton
Corydalis
Crocus, Autumn
Crown of Thorns
Cuban Laurel
Cuckoo Pint
Cutleaf Philodendron
Cycads
Cyclamen
Cypress Spurge

Daffodil
Daphne
Datura
Day Lily
Deadly Nightshade
Death Camas
Devil's Ivy
Delphinium
Decentrea

Dieffenbachia
Dog Bane
Dolls Eyes
Dracaena Palm
Dragon Tree
Duchman's Breeches
Dumb Cane
Dwarf Larkspur

Easter Flower
Easter Lily
Eggplant

Elaine
Elderberry
Elephant Ear
Emerald Duke
Emerald Feather
English Ivy
English Yew
Ergot
Eucalyptus
Euonymus
Euphorbia
Evergreen
Everlasting Pea

False Cactus
False Hellbore
Ferns
Feverfew
Fiddle-leaf fig
Fiddleneck
Florida Beauty
Flag
Flax
Fleur-de-lis
Fly Agaric
Four O'Clock

Foxglove
Foxtail Barley
Fruit Salad Plant

Geranium
German Ivy
Ghostweed
Giant Dumb Cane
Glacier Ivy
Golden Chain
Gold Dieffenbachia
Gold Dust Dracaena
Golden Chain
Golden Glow
Golden Pothos
Gopher Purge
Green Dragon
Green False Hellebore
Ground Ivy
Groundsel

Hahn's Self-Branching Ivy
Heartland Philodendron
Hellebore
Hemlock, Poison
Hemlock, Water
Henbane
Holly
Honeysuckle
Horsebeans
Horsebrush
Horse Chestnut
Horse Nettle
Horse Tail
Hurricane Plant
Hyacinth
Hydrangea

Impatiens

Indian Rubber Plant
Indian Tobacco
Indian Turnip
Inkberry
Iris
Iris Ivy

Jack in the Pulpit
Jamestown Weed
Janet Craig Dracaena
Japanese Show Lily
Jatropha
Java Beans
Jequirity Bean
Jessamine
Jerusalem Cherry
Jimsonweed
Johnsongrass
Jonquil
Jungle Trumpets
Juniper

Kalanchoe
Klamath Weed

Laburnum
Lacy Tree Philodendron
Lambkill
Lantana
Larkspur
Laurel
Lily
Lily Spider
Lily of the Valley
Lima Bean
Locoweed
Lords and Ladies
Lupine

Madagascar Dragon Tree
Majesty
Mandrake
Marble Queen
Marigold
Marijuana
Mayapple
Mescal Bean
Mexican Breadfruit
Mexican Poppy
Milk Bush
Milkweed
Milo
Miniature Croton
Mistletoe
Mock Orange
Monkshood
Moonseed
Morning Glory
Mother-in Law's Tongue
Morning Glory
Mountain Laurel
Mushrooms

Nap-at-noon
Narcissus
Needlepoint Ivy
Nephytis
Nightshade
Nutmeg

Oaks
Oleander
Onion
Oriental Lily

Panther Cap Mushroom
Parlour Ivy
Peace Lily

Peach (pits and wilting leaves)
Pencil Cactus
Pennyroyal
Peony
Periwinkle
Philodendron
Pie Plant
Pimpernel
Pin Cherry
Pinks
Plumosa Fern
Poinciana
Poinsettia
Poison Hemlock
Poison Ivy
Poison Oak
Pokeweed
Poppy
Potato
Pothos
Precatory Bean
Primrose
Privet

Quaker Bonnets

Ragwort
Red Clover
Red Emerald
Red Maple
Red Princess
Red-Margined Dracaena
Red Sage
Rhododendron
Rhubarb
Ribbon Plant
Richweed
Rosemary Pea
Rubber Plant

Saddle Leaf Philodendron
Sago Palm
Satin Pothos
Schefflera
Scotch Broom
Scouringbrush
Senecio
Sensitive Fern
Sheep Laurel
Silver Pothos
Silver Queen
Singletary Pea
Skunk Cabbage
Snake Plant
Snapdragon
Snowdrops
Snow on the Mountain
Soapwort
Sorghum
Spotted Dumb Cane
Squirrelcorn
Squirreltail Barley
St. Johnswort
Staggerweed
Star of Bethlehem
Stinging Nettle
String of Pearls
Striped Dracaena
Sudan Grass
Sweet Cherry
Sweetheart Ivy
Sweetpea
Swiss Cheese plant

Tangia Pea
Tansy Mustard
Tansy Ragwort
Taro Vine

Tarweed
Thornapple
Tiger Lily
Tinsel Tree
Tobacco
Tolguacha
Tomato Plant (green fruit, stem and leaves)
Tree Philodendron
Tri-leaf-wonder
Trillium
Tropic Snow Dieffenbachia
Trumpet Vine
Tulip
Tung Tree
Valley
Venus Flytrap
Verbena
Virginia Creeper

Walnuts
Water Hemlock
Weeping Fig
West Indian Lantana
White Clover
White Hellebore
White Sanicle
White Snakeroot
Wild Barley
Wild Black Cherry
Wild Bleeding Heart
Wild Call
Wisteria
Wolfs Bane
Wood Nettle

Yellow Jasmine
Yellow Jessamine
Yellow Oleander
Yellow Sage

Yellow Star Thistle
Yew

Source: ASPCA

**OTHER THINGS THAT ARE
POISONOUS TO CATS:**

Acetaminophen (Tylenol)
Alcohol
Antifreeze
Aromatherapy oils
(Please consult your vet before using
ANY aromatherapy oil on your cat.)
Aspirin

Bleach
Boric Acid
Brake Fluid

Cleaning Fluid
Chocolate

Coffee

Deodorants
Deodorizers

Detergent
Disinfectants
Dye

Fungicides
Furniture Polish

Garlic

Herbicides

Ibuprofen
Insecticides

Laxatives

Lead

Metal Polish
Mineral Spirits
Mothballs

Nail Polish & Remover

Onion

Paint
Paint Remover
Paracetamol
Petrol
Phenylbutazone

Photographic Developer

Rat/Ant Poison
Rubbing Alcohol

Shoe Polish
Snail/Slug Bait
Suntan Lotion

Tar
Teflon

Weedkiller
Windshield Washer Fluid
Wood Preservatives

Zinc

Source: ASPCA

SOME FLOWERS AND PLANTS THAT ARE CAT SAFE

Achillea
African Violet
Alyssum
Aster
Basil
Bean Sprouts
Begonia
Buddleia
Calendula
Celosia
Chamomile
Chervil
Chives
Cleome
Columbine
Coneflower
Coriander
Cosmos
Dahlia
Dianthus
Dill
Dorotheanthus
Forget-Me-Not
Helotrope
Hollyhock
Hyssop
Impatiens
Japanese Matatabi
Lavender
Lemon Balm
Lemon Verbena
Lettuce
Lovage
Marum
Miniature Rose
Mint

Monarda
Nasturtium
Oats
Orchid
Oregano
Pansy
Parsley
Peppermint
Petunia
Phlox
Portulaca
Roses
Rosemary
Sage
Scabiosa
Shasta Daisy
Snapdragon
Spearmint
Spider Plant
Spinach
Strawflower
Sunflower
Tarragon
Thyme
Torenia
Verbascum
Violet
Wheat
Zinnia

Source: ASPCA

Printed in Great Britain
by Amazon.co.uk, Ltd.,
Marston Gate.